IRELAND STANDING FIRM

and

EAMON DE VALERA

CLASSICS OF IRISH HISTORY
General Editor: Tom Garvin

Other titles in this series:

P. S. O'Hegarty
The Victory of Sinn Féin
with an introduction by Tom Garvin
(1998)

Walter McDonald
Some Ethical Questions of Peace and War
with an introduction by Tom Garvin
(1998)

Joseph Johnston
Civil War in Ulster
edited by Roy Johnston
(1999)

James Mullin
The Story of a Toiler's Life
edited by Patrick Maume
(2000)

IRELAND STANDING FIRM
MY WARTIME MISSION IN WASHINGTON

and

EAMON DE VALERA
A MEMOIR

Robert Brennan

with an introduction by
Richard H. Rupp

University College Dublin Press
Preas Choláiste Ollscoile Bhaile Átha Cliath

Ireland Standing Firm and *Eamon de Valera*
were first published in instalments
in the *Irish Press*, 1958
This edition first published 2002

ISBN 1 900621 68 1
ISSN 1383–6883

University College Dublin Press
Newman House, 86 St Stephen's Green
Dublin 2, Ireland
www.ucdpress.ie

Cataloguing in Publication data available from the British Library

This book is printed on acid-free paper
Typeset in Ireland in Baskerville by Elaine Shiels, Bantry, Co. Cork
Printed in England by MPG Books, Bodmin, Cornwall

CONTENTS

ACKNOWLEDGEMENTS

The text of both memoirs appeared in the *Irish Press* during the spring of 1958. To the best of my knowledge, neither has been reprinted prior to this edition. The texts exist in carbon copies of the original manuscripts, and are used with the permission of Brennan's granddaughter, Yvonne Jerrold.

I find it my pleasant duty to recognize Yvonne Jerrold of Cambridge, England, for kindly supplying me with the texts; the late Charles Justice of Blowing Rock, North Carolina, for introducing me to Robert Brennan's work; Mr. Dennis Joseph Boykin of Boone, North Carolina, who keyed *Ireland Standing Firm* for publication; Barbara Mennell of UCD Press for her encouragement and editorial assistance in the project; and Appalachian State University, Boone, North Carolina, from which I am happily retired, for giving me scholarly leave to work on the project during the autumn of 1997. My thanks to you all.

RICHARD H. RUPP
Boone, North Carolina
October, 2001

INTRODUCTION

Richard H. Rupp

Robert Brennan was a Wexford man, born 22 July 1881, to Robert and Brigid Kearney Brennan. His development as a revolutionary was gradual. His initial interest was in the language and the ancient Gaelic culture, not politics. He was first drawn into the struggle for Irish independence during the centenary celebrations for the Rebellion of 1798 when he sang a ballad in Irish. He became one of the founders of the Wexford branch of the Gaelic League, an organisation dedicated to the preservation of hurling, the Gaelic or Irish language, and native customs. (He recounts his accidental discovery of the Gaelic Revival movement and his meeting with Douglas Hyde in the early pages of his autobiography, *Allegiance*.) Brennan taught Irish to members of the Wexford branch until they were able to bring in a native Irish speaker. He was employed by Wexford County Council as Assistant County Surveyor, and cycled everywhere in the county to inspect the 400 miles of roads that were in his territory four times a year, until he left in 1909 to join the *Enniscorthy Echo* as a reporter. He was the Wexford correspondent for *The Irish Times* and also a prolific writer of short stories for magazines and newspapers.

On 6 July 1909, he married Una Bolger and over the next forty years they raised a family of three daughters named after the mythic Irish women, Emer, Maeve and Deirdre, and a son named Robert Patrick.

Brennan was County Secretary to Sinn Féin and helped to organise the Irish Republican Brotherhood in Wexford. Narrowly escaping execution for his role in the Rising of 1916, he spent the rest of that year in a succession of English prisons. He was released only to be shadowed and sought repeatedly for the next five years. During this period Brennan served as director of publicity for Sinn Féin and was director of elections for the first Dáil. He was again arrested and imprisoned in Usk Jail, Wales. Altogether he spent time in six English jails and five Irish ones. In 1920 Eamon de Valera appointed him Under Secretary for External Affairs, a position he later discharged in de Valera's first administration.

After the Civil War, Brennan was the first General Manager of the *Irish Press*. De Valera returned to power in 1932 and in 1934 Brennan became Secretary to the Irish Legation in Washington, moving there with his family in the same year. Four years later he was appointed Irish Minister to Washington, a post that he discharged with distinction from 1938 to 1947. Home again after the war at the age of 66, Robert Brennan was appointed Director of Radio Éireann. In 1948, when he was replaced by the new government, he retired from public life to concentrate on writing. He spent time on his memoirs, bringing out the first (and only) edition of *Allegiance* with his Irish publishers, Browne and Nolan, in 1950. In the same year he was appointed Director of the Irish News Agency. Over the next few years his third novel was published and he also wrote further memoirs and reminiscences that were published in the *Irish Press* between 1956 and 1958.

Robert and Una Brennan had eight grandchildren. Una died on 3 August 1958. Robert Brennan lived on another six years, dying on 13 November 1964, a faithful servant and eloquent spokesman for his fledgling nation.

Ireland Standing Firm: My Wartime Mission in Washington

Brennan's entertaining account of his time in Washington was serialised in the Irish newspaper, the *Irish Press*, in daily instalments during April and May of 1958. Early during the Second World War Winston Churchill and Franklin D. Roosevelt tried to pressure Ireland into joining the alliance against Germany, Italy, and Japan. But Brennan, upon instruction from his government, resisted. He reflected Irish opinion when he said in his memoir that "Ninety-nine per cent of the Irish are against any involvement in the war, and no government could last overnight who departed from a policy of neutrality."

Brennan's task was complex. He had to court American public opinion, to win the favour of American bishops, senators, and journalists by constantly explaining the rationale for Irish neutrality. While fruitlessly objecting to the United States government and to the world at large over the unfair partition of Ireland, he explained that Ireland was in a no-win situation, having to defend itself against the dual prospects of German aerial bombardment and British reoccupation.

On the political side, this memoir gives us glimpses of Brennan's public relations campaign. For instance, he recounts his speech at Nassau Hall, Princeton University, in which he makes an eloquent defence of Irish neutrality. Such was his job, to win over American audiences ignorant of Irish political realities, one evening at a time. After America entered the war in December 1941, his task grew harder. Churchill and Roosevelt increased pressure on the Irish. A month later, when German bombers set Belfast ablaze, Brennan defended de Valera's sending the Dublin fire brigade north as perfectly consistent with a one Ireland policy. Belfast might not be part of independent Ireland, but it was part of Ireland.

By the same reasoning Brennan vigorously protested against the stationing of American troops in Derry in 1942. Whether sparring directly with Roosevelt or indirectly with Churchill, Robert Brennan kept the strategic interests of Ireland foremost while cultivating strong and supportive relationships with American statesmen, businessmen, and churchmen. Perhaps his most difficult task was quashing rumours of a German intelligence network operating freely in Éire. One memorable encounter with the US Director of the Office of Strategic Services, William "Wild Bill" Donovan, led to a backing down by that American intelligence chief in the face of Brennan's sterling Irish logic. No network of German spies operated successfully in Dublin or elsewhere in Ireland during the war.

Such was the stuff of Brennan's wartime mission to Washington. For nine years he walked the Washington high wire, ably serving Irish interests there until 1947, when he returned to Dublin to take up the post of Director of Radio Éireann. His replacement in Washington was Robert Nunan. By this time his daughter Maeve Brennan was making her own career as a journalist and writer of short stories in New York. (Her editor and long-time friend at *The New Yorker*, William Maxwell, gives a fond and perceptive account of her career in his introduction to her posthumous volume of short stories, *The Springs of Affection*, 1997.)

We are left with this memoir of a trying time three thousand miles from home. Wry, vivid, detached yet humorous, Brennan's voice echoes though the memoir from first to last. He is a raconteur, a storyteller who begs your leave to listen a while. This memoir belongs to literature, not to history, and reads very well. May you enjoy it.

Eamon de Valera: A Memoir

The second memoir, *Eamon de Valera*, was also written for the *Irish Press*, probably in 1958. Bothered by worsening vision, de Valera was about to step down as Taoiseach. Shortly after the memoir appeared, de Valera became President of Ireland, but in the interim Brennan felt compelled to write a memoir justifying his mentor's achievement on behalf of Ireland.

Thus this memoir differs in kind and in purpose from the wartime memoir. This one makes no effort at objective history. Instead it offers us glimpses of Dev in times of crisis, anecdotal evidence of his political genius, of his absolute devotion to the cause of Irish independence, and of Brennan's warm admiration for the man. Here we see important decisions that de Valera made at moments when those who did not know him misunderstood him. Brennan writes as a friend, a colleague, and as a loyal supporter, not as a political analyst. The memoir is admittedly one sided in its purpose, to set the record straight.

We might best view *Eamon de Valera* as a collection of portraits in the long gallery of memory, each one showing a different pose, a different colouring. Plucking at our sleeve is the curator of the collection, Robert Brennan, saying "Look, look here! Now look there! See how the man grows! See his unchanging purpose in different settings through changing times!" We are indebted to Brennan for his eyewitness to history and for his graceful polemic of a man he loved. Both men gave their hearts and their lives to a nation struggling to be born. Both lived long enough to see their progeny grow to robust independence.

Whatever Eamon de Valera's final position in the judgment of historians, no one can doubt the allegiance and the loyalty that Brennan shows here. Perhaps Robert Brennan himself is due a reassessment. A modest monument to his memory in Wexford would be a good place to start. I have enjoyed getting to know the man through his work, and I hope that you will too.

A CHRONOLOGY OF ROBERT BRENNAN

22 JULY 1881 Robert Brennan is born in Wexford.

SUMMER 1898 Brennan leaves Christian Brothers' school in Wexford and starts work in the office of the Wexford County Surveyor. Over the next few years, through evening study, he qualifies as a surveyor, gaining his certificate at the Royal University, Dublin.

1906 Brennan is appointed Assistant County Surveyor in Wexford.

6 MAY 1909 Robert Brennan marries Una Bolger (*née* Anastasia Bolger) of Wexford, who was among the first members of Cumann na mBan and was one of the three women who raised the flag in Enniscorthy in the 1916 Rising.

1909 A few months after his marriage, Brennan resigns as surveyor and joins the *Enniscorthy Echo* as a reporter.

EASTER 1916 Brennan is one of the leaders of the Rising in Wexford. He surrenders his command, is tried in Dublin, sentenced to be shot, and imprisoned at George Street Barracks, Wexford; then successively at Waterford Jail; Kilmainham Jail, Dublin; Mountjoy Prison, Dublin; Dartmoor Prison, Devon; Lewes Jail, Sussex; Parkhurst Prison, Isle of Wight; Pentonville Prison, London; Usk Prison, Wales; Arbor Hill Prison, Dublin; and Gloucester Prison, Gloucester, at various intervals during the next three years.

1917 Daughter Maeve is born. Brennan is re-arrested and sent to Cork Prison, where he goes on a hunger strike.

1918–21 Brennan becomes Director of Publicity for Sinn Féin and Director of Elections to establish the first Dáil.

1920 Eamon de Valera appoints Brennan Under Secretary for External Affairs for Dáil Éireann.

1921 Brennan's novel, *The False Fingertip*, is published in Dublin under the pen name of Selskar Kearney.

6 DECEMBER 1921 The Anglo-Irish Treaty is signed in London.

3 JANUARY 1922 The Treaty is submitted to Dáil Éireann.

7 JANUARY 1922 The Dáil approves the Treaty by a vote of 64 to 57.

9 JANUARY 1922 De Valera resigns as President and stands for re-election. He is defeated by Arthur Griffith, 60–58.

JANUARY 1922 Brennan organises the Irish Race Congress in Paris to support independence.

MARCH 1922 The IRA organises resistance to the Treaty and elects an executive board of sixteen to support total independence from Great Britain.

APRIL 1922 Rory O'Connor seizes the Four Courts in Dublin; de Valera and Michael Collins patch up their differences, aided by Brennan.

22 JUNE 1922 IRA gunmen assassinate Sir Henry Wilson in London.

27 JUNE 1922 The Free State government demands that O'Connor surrender the Four Courts. O'Connor refuses, so the army under General Richard Mulcahy attacks with British artillery. The Irish Civil War begins.

JULY 1922 Brennan becomes Director of Publicity for the Republicans.

12 AUGUST 1922 Arthur Griffith dies of strain and overwork in Dublin.

23 AUGUST 1922 Michael Collins, newly elected President of the Executive Council by the Dáil, is ambushed and

killed in County Cork. Brennan goes underground and spends time in France under an assumed name.

27 APRIL 1923 De Valera decides that further resistance to the Treaty is futile and surrenders.

27 AUGUST 1923 De Valera is arrested.

JULY 1924 De Valera is released from prison. Back in Dublin, Brennan is organising and fundraising for de Valera's new Republican newspaper.

1926 Fianna Fáil founded by de Valera. Brennan's novel, *The Toledo Dagger*, is published in London.

JUNE 1927 Fianna Fáil wins 44 of 153 seats in the Dáil but refuses to occupy them in protest over the Oath of Fidelity to the British Crown.

JULY 1927 Finance Minister Kevin O'Higgins is assassinated.

AUGUST 1927 De Valera takes Oath of Fidelity to the British Crown and leads Fianna Fáil into Dáil.

1930 Brennan's play about convict life in an English prison, *The Bystander*, is performed at the Abbey Theatre in Dublin to an enthusiastic response which leads to its being revived for a further week in December.

Also during the 1930s Brennan's play, *Goodnight Mr. O'Donnell*, a comedy based on the never-explained disappearance of the Irish crown jewels from Dublin Castle at the start of the century, is performed at the Dublin Olympia with Jimmy O'Dea.

1931 Brennan becomes General Manager of the *Irish Press*.

FEBRUARY 1932 Fianna Fáil forms a government and elects de Valera President of the Executive Council (Prime Minister).

1934 Brennan appointed Secretary to the Irish Legation in Washington, DC.

26 AUGUST 1938 Brennan appointed Irish Minister to the United States.

1 SEPTEMBER 1939 Germany invades Poland. World War II begins.

15 AUGUST 1945 World War II ends.

26 FEBRUARY 1947 Brennan returns to Dublin, becoming Director of Radio Éireann.

1950 Brennan is appointed Director of the Irish News Agency. His autobiography, *Allegiance*, is published in Dublin.

1951 Brennan's novel, *The Man Who Walked Like a Dancer*, is published in London.

1956 and 1957 Brennan's weekly column of reminiscences 'Mainly Meandering' is published in the *Irish Press.*

1958 Brennan's memoirs are serialized in the *Irish Press.*

3 AUGUST 1958 Una Brennan, Robert's wife, dies in Dublin.

13 NOVEMBER 1964 Robert Brennan dies in Dublin.

IRELAND STANDING FIRM

MY WARTIME MISSION IN WASHINGTON

Robert Brennan in Washington D. C.

I have frequently been asked to write the story of my experiences in America during the Second World War. I hesitated to do so because I kept no diary during the period, but lately on reading *The Memoirs of Cordell Hull*[1] I came across many statements regarding Ireland's attitude towards the war which are, I won't say biased, but misinformed, and I thought that in justice to the good name of my country I should put on record the Irish point of view on the many contentious issues raised. Such a record may be helpful to Ireland in the unpredictable future.

I was appointed Minister to the United States about a year before the war started, and I served in that capacity all through the war. As most of what I am going to say concerns the question of Ireland's neutrality, I should remind the reader that under the clauses of the Treaty of 1922, it was provided that the British continued to occupy certain ports in Cork and Donegal and that in time of war or strained relations with a foreign power they could occupy not merely these but any other Irish port which seemed necessary to them.

This meant, of course, that if England became engaged in a war, Ireland would also automatically be in it. It is true to say that if any such war had broken out between 1922 and 1937, we would have been committed to it on England's side. It is true also, of course, that in such an event the Irish government could have declared our neutrality, but the fact that the British had full use of our ports would have made a mockery of such a declaration.

However, as God had it to be, there was no such war between 1922 and 1937, and when the war did start in 1939, it appeared that we had barely got out under the wire.

1 Cordell Hull with Andrew Berding, *The Memoirs of Cordell Hull*, 2 vols (New York: Macmillan, 1948).

In February 1932 Eamon de Valera, having been ten years in the wilderness, was returned to power. He had been advised that the land annuities were due not to the British but to the Irish Exchequer. I do not propose here to go into the question more fully than to state that the land annuities were sums paid by Irish farmers for the privilege of becoming owners of the land for which they had previously paid rent as tenants. Before the General Election of 1932 de Valera had stated that if elected he would hold the annuities and not pay them into the British Exchequer as had been previously done and when he won the election he refused to transfer the monies to England. They amounted at the time to five or six million pounds per annum. The British thereupon imposed on Irish cattle exported to England a penal tariff with the object of extracting from the Irish sufficient money to recoup them for the loss of the annuities. The Irish government's reply was to impose certain restrictive tariffs on British imports.

Thus began the so-called economic war which inflicted considerable damage on both countries and which in course of time was to result in a victory for Ireland because the Irish government stood firm and the farmers in the main stood by the government. When he embarked on the annuities war, not even de Valera could have foreseen that its ultimate outcome would bring far more beneficial results to Ireland than a mere victory over the annuities. It was to eventuate in our winning the power to declare and maintain Ireland's neutrality in all England's future wars.

The economic war lasted for six years at the end of which time it was clear that both countries were sick of it. They decided to negotiate and it was lucky for all concerned that England had a statesman at the helm and Ireland another. The men were Neville Chamberlain and Eamon de Valera.

On the eve of the negotiations I happened to be in Ireland and I was surprised to find that de Valera was confident that not only would he win from the British a settlement favourable to Ireland on the annuities question, but that he could persuade them to rewrite certain clauses in the Treaty of 1921 which were vital from the Irish point of view. Above all he hoped he would get the British to evacuate the ports they held in Cork and Donegal and that they would surrender the rights they held to occupy any other of our ports in time of danger or of war.

I had discussed this question with several of the members of Dev's cabinet, and they all agreed with me that in the negotiations, while he might win on the annuities, he would find the British adamant on the ports. I told de Valera that he would lose on the question of the ports.

"Why do you think so?" he asked.

"Well, after all, the annuities amount to a small thing for the British, but the ports are vital to them," and I went on to refer to the fact that Roger Casement in his pamphlet "Ireland, Germany and the Next War", written just before the First World War, had so stated. Kuno Meyer in his pamphlet "Ireland, Germany, and the Freedom of the Seas" had made the same point.

"If I were Chamberlain," I said, "I would give you all, or more than you want on the question of annuities, but I would hold on to the ports."

In the upshot he won Chamberlain to his view. In the agreement he then secured, the British gave up the ports in Cork and Donegal and they also abandoned their claims to the occupation of the other Irish ports in the twenty-six counties. Had they not done so, Ireland would inevitably have been in the war. Irish people who are not yet, say, 25 years old might be excused from not knowing this, but many who are older seem to have forgotten the fact that it was the statesmanship of de Valera which saved Ireland from being involved in the Second World War.

I went to America in the spring of 1934 as Secretary of the Irish Legation at Washington and by the time I was appointed Minister in 1938, I had many friends in the United States Congress. Early on I had come to the conclusion that if it came to a world conflict, America would be found on the side of Britain. I realised, too, that if Ireland was to be kept out of the conflict, we would have to rely very largely on Ireland's friends in America and particularly on such friends as we had in the U.S. Congress.

It was clear to me in 1938 that war was in the offing and that if it broke out, America would eventually be found in the line-up against the Axis powers. The American press was solid against Hitler, not merely because of his rattling the sword, but because of his treatment of the Jews. The so-called peace settlement at Munich at the expense of Czechoslovakia, though it was welcomed by the administration, was generally condemned by the American people, to a far greater extent than it was in England or France.

I was a guest at the Gridiron Club Dinner, an annual event organised by the Washington pressmen, where there was presented a tableau showing Neville Chamberlain with his umbrella returning from Munich, triumphantly crying: "Peace for our time". He was confronted by a portrait of Disraeli and he asked who it was. The reply brought down the house. "He was one of the very great prime ministers of England. He was a Jew."

This brings me to a few of the many contradictions one finds in America. Traditionally the great bulk of the people are isolationists and they were particularly so at the time of which I am writing. Their attitude was that if the Europeans wanted to indulge in wars, that was Europe's concern, but they would have none of it. Their spokesmen and their newspapers, however, loudly told the Europeans what and what not to do. I mentioned this contradiction to an American friend of mine who was in the administration, and he said,

"I know. I have always thought we are the greatest kibitzers in the world." (A kibitzer—a Jewish word, I think—has much the same meaning as "the hurler on the ditch".)

While, as I say, the vast mass of the Americans were genuinely isolationist, the administration, including the government and the armed services, were convinced that the British Empire was a bulwark for the American system. While they deplored colonialism and despised the pukka sahib, they also genuinely feared that the downfall of the Empire would create world problems for them which they had no way of solving.

Added to this there was the universal American admiration for achievement. They themselves had achieved in a remarkably short time the conquest of a continent and they could not, in spite of two wars waged against Britain, withhold their admiration for a people who from a small island located on the perimeter of Europe had achieved the conquest of almost the whole world.

Then again I found that even in the most select circles, particularly in Washington, which after all is the capital of the U.S., there was an uneasy feeling that vis à vis the English gentleman, they had not yet arrived. Not all of them could have their daughters presented at the Court of St. James, but at least they could manoeuvre an invitation to the British Embassy in Washington, and such an invitation conferred on them a social cachet which lasted all their lives. As late as 1936, a lady called on me in connection with something to do with her husband's estate. Her husband was the son of an Irish-American who was a good friend to Ireland. All I knew of the lady was what I had heard from many of her friends, that she had once danced with the Prince of Wales. During the conversation, which was on very mundane matters, the lady mentioned at least three times that she had once danced with the Prince of Wales.

The British knew very well what an asset they had in the monarchy and, indeed, in the whole feudal system. Everyone they sent to their Embassy in Washington, if he had not a title, was at least in line to have one. They patronised the Americans and the Americans lapped it up.

It is not of course only the Americans who fall flat on their faces for royalty or near royalty. In Republican France I had earlier seen the proletariat go wild with enthusiasm for le Prince de Galles.

At the time of the visit of the British King and Queen [George VI and Elizabeth] to Washington, I discussed this matter of worship of royalty with a friend of mine, an Irish-American whose wife was blazing with indignation because she had not got an invitation to the garden party at the British Embassy. I said it was difficult to understand such an attitude on the part of people so ultra-democratic as the Americans. His reply was that the Irish were as king-minded as any and reminded me that Parnell was called the uncrowned King of Ireland and that a popular song he had heard on a visit to

Ireland was "We'll crown de Valera King of Ireland". I then recollected that at the Ard Fheis of Sinn Féin in 1917, when there was some doubt as to the ultimate objectives of the organisation, the newly elected President said that the only proviso about the King, if we decided to have one, was that he would not come from the House of Windsor.

To get back to the American scene in 1938, I decided that all in all, if it came to war, America would be found on the British side, passively at first and actively later on, and I saw that the task I had representing a country which was determined to remain neutral would be no easy one. I had to aid me two very important factors. The first was that the American administration of the time was a Democratic one, which meant that the Irish were far more powerful than they would have been had the administration been Republican. The second was that the Irish in the United States were, with few exceptions, wholeheartedly with us in the desire that Ireland should be free to make her own choice.

Here is a seeming contradiction. When America goes to war, all her people believe that their cause is a holy one. They are in the war not for territorial gain, or for empire. They had consciously rejected whatever imperial designs Theodore Roosevelt may have had and having taken the Philippines and Cuba from the Spanish, they had set both free. They are fighting for freedom and democracy and against tyranny, dictatorship and authoritarianism. Crusaders fighting in a holy cause, they wonder why every right-thinking country is not on their side. In all of this the Irish in America are in the forefront. They are the first to join up and the first to die.

When it comes to Ireland, the Irish in the United States, in the main, take another point of view. The readily accept the argument that Ireland is not free to decide since her ancient territory is still in part occupied by the invader. In any case, they say history showed that America had always fought for freedom, including the freedom of any country to decide the question of peace or war for itself. Therefore the Irish people had the right to decide whether or not they would go to war, and the decision of the Irish people was what mattered.

Before the war started I had, as I say, made many friends in Congress, including Senators Jim Murray of Montana, Francis Moloney of Connecticut, Joseph O'Mahony of Wyoming, Pat McCarran of Nevada, Jim Meade of New York, and many others. In addition, I had many friends in the House of Representatives including John McCormack, who during all the period of stress held the key position of House Majority Leader, meaning that he was the man in the House of Representatives who had the job of lining up the Congressmen in support of such measures as the President wanted passed. Because of his position he had the entrée to the White House at any time. John McCormack was very good at all times, and I never once experienced a refusal from him when I asked him to intervene on Ireland's behalf. We had many other friends in the House of Representatives, but outstanding was Jim McGranery of Philadelphia. What Ireland owes to this man can never be repaid. Though he was a loyal and staunch member of the Democratic Party, he was fearless to a rare degree, and he stood up to friend and foe alike in defence of Ireland's rights, even at a time when it was anything but popular to do so.

Early on I had used my experience as a newspaperman to establish good relations with the press. As soon as I became Minister, I visited the offices of the chief newspapers in New York, Washington, Chicago, San Francisco and Los Angeles. I was on easy terms with Arthur Krock of the *New York Times*, Geoffrey Parsons and Joe Driscoll of the *New York Herald Tribune*, Felix Morley and Edward Ffolliot of the *Washington Post*, Charlie Lucey of the *Scripps Howard Press*, Kingsbury Smith of the Hearst chain, and a host of others. My wife, who has a knack of making and keeping friends, was in constant touch with Betty Hynes of the *Washington Times Herald*, Mrs. Hope Ridings Miller of the *Post*, Evelyn Peyton Gordon of the *Washington News*, Miss Brooks of the *Washington Star*, and, indeed, with dozens of others. Ed Keating, the Editor of *Labor*, who had the ear of every senator and congressman from the Middle West, and his wife, whom we had previously known as Nora Connolly, were intimate friends of ours, as was also

Frank Hall, the Editor of *The National Catholic Welfare Conference Bulletin*, which was sent out weekly to every Catholic paper in the United States. They were all of great help to us when, as it seemed, disaster threatened Ireland.

From the outset I had made up my mind that while, of course, staying clear of American politics, I should keep close to the leaders of the Democratic Party. There were times when the isolationists among the Republicans, seeing the drift of American foreign policy towards war, would have liked to use us against the Democratic regime. I purposely and deliberately avoided them and old friends of mine in the U.S. Republican camp, like Senator Danaher of Connecticut and Congressman Dick Walsh of California, no doubt wondered why they were not asked oftener to our house. But I had to see that Ireland was not involved in the war, and with a wily customer such as F.D.R. turned out to be I had to tread carefully.

Before the war actually started, I had made up my mind that no matter how many neutrality acts the American Congress enacted, Roosevelt would get America into the war before it ended. As it transpired, he himself was violating the spirit if not the letter of the American neutrality laws long before America was officially in the war.

De Valera planned a visit to the United States in the spring of 1939. The visit was to coincide with the opening of the New York World Fair on 30 April. My instructions were to arrange an itinerary which would enable him to visit every city and town in which he had previously been welcomed. The visit was cancelled at the last moment because of the British threat of conscription in the North of Ireland. Instead of Dev, Sean T. O'Ceallaigh, who was then the Tanaiste, arrived and he duly opened the Irish Exhibition at the World's Fair. One incident of that event remains clearly in my mind. It was a demonstration of the showmanship of the colourful Fiorello La Guardia, Mayor of New York. Just before the proceedings opened, the Mayor showed me a telegram he had had from de Valera in reply to one of his.

Later, when the Mayor was speaking to the assemblage, he said he had sent a message to President de Valera voicing the good wishes of his many friends in America, and he was expecting a reply at any moment. At this stage the speaker's words were drowned out by the roar of a motorcycle tearing down the main highway towards the meeting. The machine pulled up in a cloud of dust, and a uniformed police officer stepped off it, climbed the platform, and smartly saluting the Mayor, handed him a telegram. La Guardia tore it open, glanced at it and then, turning to the audience, cried:

"I told you I was expecting a message from Eamon de Valera. Here it is."

And he proceeded to read the telegram which he had shown me an hour earlier. The crowd was wildly enthusiastic. I heard Charlie Connolly, the Editor of the *Irish Echo*, who was sitting in the front row, saying:

"Begob, he's a master," a tribute to the mayor's showmanship. La Guardia was, however, a very sincere friend and he was very helpful at a critical time, as I shall show.

Next day, Sean T., John Hearne, and myself were received by the President. As usual Roosevelt did practically all the talking for the twenty minutes the interview lasted. I was to hear this talk many times during the coming years as F.D.R. said practically the same thing to every Irish visitor he saw. He said he was always glad to meet someone from Ireland. He had a warm corner in his heart for Ireland. His first visit to Ireland had been to Cobh during the World War when he was Assistant Secretary of the Navy. There had been some trouble at the time because the American sailors had taken the girls away from the local boys, and as a result some of them had been attacked on the streets. He, F.D.R., had found a quantity of nuts and bolts under a piece of sacking on one of the ships and discovered that it was ammunition for a counter-attack which the sailors were planning. He thought this was very funny indeed. He recalled the fact that when de Valera arrived in America in 1919 to raise his loan, he had been stumped because of the Blue Sky Laws. It was he, F.D.R., who found a way to get around the law. It was he, too, who was instrumental in getting John Quinn to visit Ireland in the summer of 1921, a step which led directly to the Truce and to the Treaty.

Sean T., the perfect diplomat at all times, said that the Irish people were fully aware of all that the President had done for Ireland and they were heartily thankful that they had his good-will, and so on. General Watson, the President's Secretary, had a few friendly words with us when seeing us off the premises. It was characteristic of Sean T. that a few weeks later he sent me a case of Irish whisky liqueur for General Watson.

An Irish group in Chicago had planned an Irish Race Convention to be held in Chicago to coincide with Mr. de Valera's projected visit. It was hoped from this to establish a nation-wide organisation to embrace all existing Irish organisations. Sean T. deputised for Dev and we had also with us John Hearne and Sean Moylan, as well as Garth Healy, our consul in Chicago. Mr. Hicks, the manager of the Morrison Hotel, had placed at Sean T's disposal a vast suite of rooms. He had given me another—all free of charge. My suite consisted of seven bedrooms and a large reception room. Sean Moylan in a letter to my wife said that I had seven bathrooms and a place to wash my hands and face.

The Convention was run by a group consisting mainly of very energetic young people who had a great deal of enthusiasm but very little experience. Before we got to Chicago they had fumbled the ball rather badly. One of the men behind the movement was Roger Faherty, the founder and president of the Irish Fellowship Club of Chicago. His father had been "a member of the cabinet" in the regime of Big Bill Thompson, the famous Mayor of Chicago who said he would like "to bust King George in the snoot". Big Bill was a Republican, and during his period of office Faherty senior, a building contractor, had practically rebuilt the magnificent Michigan Boulevard which fronts Lake Michigan.

Roger Faherty, a quiet, cultured, dignified man though he was a Republican himself, hated the political hurly-burly and genuinely wanted to see the Irish cause in America lifted above the turmoil of American politics. So when the Irish Race Convention project was put to him, he heartily fell in with the idea and, indeed, largely financed the initial steps to bring it about.

Chicago at this time was run by a political machine which was referred to by its opponents as the Kelly-Nash Gang. Kelly was the mayor and Tom Nash the power behind the throne. Their machine ruled Cook County, which includes Chicago, and they dominated politics in the whole state of Illinois, which they held for the Democratic Party.

As soon as we arrived in Chicago, I knew that we were in for trouble. An elderly lady, whom I knew to be a member of the committee, collared me on the railway platform and asked me if they had not done right in excluding Roger Faherty from the proceedings. I was completely bewildered and I gave her an evasive reply.

Later, I learned that Mayor Kelly had told the Committee that if Roger Faherty appeared on the platform, he, the Mayor, would not be there. So they had told Roger that he was not to take part, though, indeed, later on, they had to call on him to pay some of the bills, which he very generously did.

That was not all. A deputation consisting of ten or twelve people, all of whom had given good service to the Irish cause, called on Sean T. and myself. Most of them were known to Sean T. by their first names. Their spokesman stated that everyone connected with the organising of the Convention was tied up with the Kelly Nash gang and that . . . At this stage Sean T. interrupted the speaker and said coldly that we had not come there to discuss the party politics of America, and he refused to hear anything further on the matter. The members of the deputation thereupon trailed out rather disconsolately.

In spite of all this, the Convention put up a good front. There were delegates from most of the American cities and from nearly every Irish organisation in the States. A central committee was elected to direct Irish activities in the United States.

At the final rally we had a really good speech from that old warrior for Irish rights, Joe Scott of Los Angeles, and one that really thrilled the audience from Sean Moylan.

At Chicago, I left my friends who were returning to New York. I took the train, not for Washington, but for the West Coast.

The reason for this was that the British King and Queen were scheduled to visit Washington. At that time the position of the Irish Minister in Washington was anomalous. In British eyes he was in the Empire. In the eyes of the Irish he was not. This was because people generally do not understand the meaning of External Association, the plan put forward by de Valera in an endeavour to reconcile the other sides in the Treaty debates. Between 1932 and 1938 he had by successive measures actually achieved this status. This set-up is exemplified today by India, which though an independent republic is still associated with the British Commonwealth.

That, in effect, was the position of Ireland in 1939, the time I am dealing with. My credentials as Minister were signed not by Eamon de Valera but by King George and, indeed, as late as 1947 my successor was left cooling his heels in Washington for three months before he could present his credentials because King George was not available to sign them. The position is, of course, different today.

At any rate I decided that I was not going to be in the line-up with the representatives of the British Dominions to be received by the King and Queen on the dais in front of the British Embassy.

There had been a couple of occasions when I had been placed in an embarrassing position in this respect. For instance, there had been a funeral which was attended by all the heads of missions in Washington. I received a notice to the effect that the British and Dominion representatives would assemble at the British Embassy and walk to the Cathedral in a body. Instead, my wife and I drove directly to the Cathedral. Notwithstanding that, I found that we had been seated not according to protocol but amongst the British representatives.

Dublin agreed that I should absent myself during the royal visit and directed me to travel to San Francisco and intermediate points to thank all the people who had set up committees to welcome de Valera. Which is what I did.

Prior to this, however, there had occurred an incident in connection with the visit which gave me the opportunity of saving the British Ambassador, Sir Ronald Lindsay, some embarrassment. He was a very decent man who was somewhat shy and awkward and we had become friendly in an atmosphere in which each of us frankly recognised the difficulties inherent in the anomalous position of the Irish Legation of which I have spoken. A short time before this he had quite gratuitously saved me from walking into what might have been an awkward situation in connection with the visit of a British battleship to Washington and I was glad of a chance to repay him. Also I had made up my mind that I should establish a friendly personal relationship with the personnel at the Embassy and I am glad to say that I succeeded in doing this at all times.

The incident I speak of came about at a dinner in the Mayflower Hotel. It was given by Mr. William Jeffars, the President of the Union Pacific Railway, to celebrate the premiere of the picture *Union Pacific*, which told the story of the building of the railway, the completion of which was the culminating point in the struggle to conquer the frontier and unite the eastern and western sections of the continent. The railway was built largely by Irish labourers, of whom Bill Jeffars's father was one. Bill was naturally proud of the fact that the son of a man who had been a labourer on the railway that crossed the Great Divide was now the president of that great transportation system. He was also very proud of his Irish origin.

The guests at the dinner party consisted of the senators of all the states through which the railway ran, and their wives. Owing to the large part the Irish had played in its building, the Irish Minister and his wife were the guests of honour. Everything was going smoothly at the dinner until a senator's wife suggested that it would be a good idea to organise a movement in the Senate to block everything the English wanted. Another senator's wife joined her, and soon the discussion became general; all the ladies agreed that the suggestion was an excellent one and that they should get at it right away. It transpired that the ladies' anger was due to the fact that they had not been invited to the garden party to be given at the Embassy on the occasion of the royal visit.

The next day I got to thinking of this. I realised, of course, that someone had blundered and I was certain that before the event took place all the senators and their wives would have been invited. I was anxious, however, to save Sir Ronald from embarrassment, so the next day I told him of what had happened the night before. To my amazement, he seemed to think that I was trying to get some more people into the garden party.

"It can't be done," he said. "Already we have issued invitations to two thousand people and that is all we can accommodate. There are thousands of people who would like to be there, but we must refuse them."

"Listen," I said, "so far as I am concerned, I don't care a hoot if there are only ten people there, or ten thousand, but you will have to have the members of the Senate and their wives."

"My good man," he said, blandly, "I consulted the State Department about this and they said it was necessary to invite only the Chairman of the Foreign Relations Committee of the Senate and his wife."

"All right," I said, rising, "On your head be it."

"Wait, wait," he said. "I know you would not have come here without a good reason. Please let me hear what you have to say."

Now this was in the early summer of 1939, and the British, seeing war in the offing, had been clamouring for supplies of various kinds. I said to Sir Ronald:

"Tomorrow you will be asking the U.S. government for something. Suppose you find that your demands are blocked in the Senate; how will you feel? You say you can accommodate only two thousand people in the garden party. The senators and their wives number less than two hundred. If you are wise, you had better make room for them."

Some six weeks later, when I came back from the West, the first caller I had was Sir Ronald Lindsay. He wanted to thank me for my advice about the garden party. He said that as soon as I had left him six weeks before, he had sent out invitations to all the senators and their wives. On the following morning the Vice President, John Nance Garner, had telephoned to him inviting him to lunch in the Senate Office Building. On arrival he found not only Mr. Gardner but half a dozen senators who were all very anxious to know why they and their wives had not received invitations to the garden party.

"I said to them," Sir Ronald told me, "that they must put the blame on the U.S. postal service for the non-delivery of the invitations, which as I knew had been sent out." He added looking at me, "Thanks, old man. But for you I would have been in the soup."

The significance of my absence from Washington during the royal visit had not gone unnoticed by the Washington columnists. They had made great fun of the fact. It was only later that I learned that the King had taken umbrage at the fact that I was not present. His Majesty had visited the New York World's Fair and in the course of his peregrinations he had come to the Irish Pavilion. Here he was received by Leo McCauley, our Consul General in New York, who it appears had been introduced to him as the Irish Minister. Leo, who of course is a very conscientious man, was showing the King the various exhibits, when he thought it incumbent on him to tell His Majesty that he was not the Irish Minister but the Consul General.

The King turned to him and said:

"And where is the Irish Minister? Why is he not here?"

This goes to show that in the summer of 1939 I was in the unique position of being the only person on the whole American continent whom the King asked for.

While I was off in the West, my wife was having her own trials. Almost every day Lady Lindsay, the wife of the Ambassador, called on her to pour out her troubles in connection with the royal visit. She was an American, a very forthright one, and she had come to be very friendly with Una and me. Now she was besieged with appeals from everyone she had ever known for invitations to the various functions in the Embassy. Already they had issued invitations to three hundred more people than the Garden could hold and they had great difficulty in getting out the tens of thousands of refusals they had to send. "She actually cried on my shoulder," said Una.

On this visit to the West I avoided publicity and for this reason I had to restrain the civic authorities and various Irish groups from giving receptions, dinners, etc., in my honour. On the train from San Francisco to Los Angeles, however, I came in for a good deal of attention. The reason was that our Consul in San Francisco, Mat Murphy, in booking my seat in the train had described me as the Irish Minister. I did not know this until the conductor came along and shook me warmly by the hand. His name was Kinsella and his people came from Tipperary. He deluged me with questions about Ireland and at Santa Barbara, where the train stopped for ten minutes, he brought along his father who was the driver of the train, to have a chat with me. The conductor must have passed the word along because as soon as the train began to move again, dozens of passengers crowded into the carriage, all eager to show their good will to Ireland's representative. It was quite a demonstration. Amongst the visitors was a very large man who introduced himself as Dudley Field Malone. I recognised the name as that of one who had been prominent in the Irish movement in the States. Some months later I saw a film in which he played the part of the British Prime Minister, Winston Churchill, and he played it very well.

On the return journey I stopped off at Omaha to thank the Chairman of the De Valera Reception Committee there, none other than Frank Matthews, who died in 1953 while holding the post of American Ambassador to Ireland. I also called on Mr. de Valera's old friend, Father Judge, who said I should not leave Omaha without calling on Sister Mary Brennan of, I think, the Sisters of Mercy. She was a daughter of Joseph Brennan, the '48 man, and a niece of the '67 man, John Savage, the ballad writer. She was close on a hundred. So I called at the convent and was told she was ill in bed. I was about to take my leave when someone said I was to wait because the Sister was getting up. She had insisted on doing so when she heard I was there.

She came down the stairs, a tiny, frail old woman, and she could hardly speak, so great was her emotion when she took my hand. We chatted for a while, and then she astonished me with this question:

"Tell me," she said, "am I right in thinking that de Valera is a Fenian?"

"Of course you're right," I said.

"Thanks be to God," she said fervently. "Now I can die happy."

During my absence in the West I missed an international incident. On 10 or 11 June, Joe McGarrity of Philadelphia, a doughty champion of the Irish cause, and Sean Russell, who of course was an Irish citizen, had been arrested in Detroit, and the Legation had received a cable with instructions that the matter was to be inquired into. Before anything could be done, however, it appeared that Congressman Jim McGranery, a personal friend of McGarrity's, had stormed into the State Department demanding to know why the so and so the men had been arrested. He was told that it was a precautionary measure to protect the British King and Queen, who were in the vicinity somewhere across the border in Canada.

"Did they say," asked Jim, "that they did not even know the King and Queen were in the neighbourhood?"

"They did, but we can't take a chance."

"Listen," said Jim. "If they didn't know those people were there, they didn't know. There's more truth and sincerity in their little fingers than there is in the whole carcase of . . .".

I won't repeat the rest of this sentence of Jim's. But he went on to say:

"Where are your brains? Don't you know that if Sean Russell wanted to bump off the King, he could do it far more easily nearer home? Let the two men out, or I'll make a laughing stock of the lot of you."

The two men were let out. Incidentally there was a cable from Pat McCartan, addressed to me personally, telling me it was my immediate duty to see that Sean Russell was released. It arrived, I was told, after the two men had been let out.

The 20th of August 1939 was a sweltering day. My family was having a holiday on the beach at Margate, New Jersey. I had spent the weekend with them and I was hurrying back to Washington. I had to change trains at Philadelphia, and as I waited for the down train, oblivious of the stifling heat, my mind was still in a whirl about what I had read in the morning papers. It was incredible that Hitler, the arch enemy of Communism, and Stalin, the arch enemy of Fascism, had the day before signed a trade agreement. Not only that, but the agreement had been signed at a time when there were French and British military missions conferring in Moscow. It was utterly incredible, but there it was, and my mind told me that it portended far more than a trade agreement. As a matter of fact, the first shots fired in World War Two were only twelve days off, but even I with all my prescience, could not foresee this.

The train thundered in, came to a halt and I got in only to find that I was sitting in front of Sir Ronald Lindsay, who was reading a magazine.

"What do you think of it?" I asked.

"Of what?"

"Of this trade agreement between Stalin and Hitler."

"Oh," he said, "it does not mean a thing. It's just a trade agreement. Do you mind, old man, if I finish reading this article? It's about some new things the archaeologists have found in Egypt."

Four days later Hitler and Stalin signed their ten years non-aggression treaty and a week later the Second World War began.

The war started with the German invasion of Poland on 1 September 1939, and two days later Britain and France declared war on Germany. On instructions I called to the State Department and gave formal notice that Ireland intended to remain neutral. Judge Moore, one of the assistant secretaries, always very friendly, expressed the hope that Ireland would be able to remain out of the war, but he seemed to doubt it. I assured him that we would take all possible steps to safeguard our neutrality and that we would resist any infringement of it from any quarter. The understanding and friendly attitude of Judge Moore was not shared by some other officials of the

State Department, who seemed to think that we should be with Britain in the fight and that the only reason we were not was because of our deep-rooted hatred of Britain.

These particular officials were always courteous and polite—except on one notable occasion—but they had the ingrained belief that in all we did we were motivated by our antagonism to England. For instance, about a year before the war started, I was instructed to inquire whether we could secure ten or twelve revenue cutters for the protection of the Irish fishing grounds. These revenue cutters had been used by the American authorities in their operations against the rum runners during Prohibition. They were exceedingly fast boats of maybe ten tons and after Prohibition ended in 1933 many of them were lying idle. Our Government had learned that they were being sold at a low price.

Joe Greene, the State Department official who looked after sales of munitions, ships, etc., to foreign governments, thought that we would have no difficulty in getting as many of these boats as we wanted and said he would take the matter up immediately with the proper authority, which, in this case, was the Treasury. When a couple of weeks had gone by I asked Joe what was happening. He said that the Navy had to be consulted and that there would be some delay. The matter dragged on for six months, and I was then told that all the parties to the Naval Agreement in 1922 had to be consulted before any such vessel could be transferred to another flag. It was clear then that there was no intention of letting us have those revenue cutters. It was considerably later when I learned that the real reason for the decision was that a fear had been voiced in some quarters that we would use these craft to attack the British Navy! Believe it or not.

Prior to the outbreak of war I had had only one serious set-to with the State Department. About the middle of April 1939 the newspapers carried an announcement to the effect that President Roosevelt had sent a message to Hitler asking him to give an undertaking that he would not attack some thirty nations which he mentioned. This was intended to be an answer to Hitler's complaint that he was being encircled by enemies. The President said that if Hitler gave the required undertaking, he (the President) would then proceed to get a similar undertaking from the other countries that they would not attack Germany. In the countries listed, Great Britain and Ireland appeared as a unit. I was instructed to protest against this, so I saw Mr. Moffat, who was at that time the Assistant Secretary of State in charge of European affairs. He said that the bracketing of Great Britain and Ireland had obviously been a typist's error and that there had been no intention to ignore the independence of Ireland. He asked me to convey this to my government, and if they were not satisfied he would issue an explanation to the press.

The reply from Dublin was to the effect that it could not have been a typist's error because they had heard Mr. Roosevelt on the air and he had used the phrase. I knew this was not correct because Roosevelt had not gone on the air with this message. However, I went to the State Department to make a further protest and was surprised to find that Mr. Moffat already had a typed draft of a reply on his desk to a planted question which the Secretary of State would answer at his press conference that day. The question was in effect:

"In his telegram to Hitler the President used the phrase 'Great Britain and Ireland'. Does this mean that the President ignores the existence of the Irish government?"

The answer was to the effect that not merely did the President not ignore the existence of the Irish government, but that the U.S. had recognised the existence of such government by accrediting to it a Minister Plenipotentiary and Envoy Extraordinary, and they had also received from Ireland a Minister Plenipotentiary and Envoy Extraordinary who was empowered to represent the Irish Free State on American soil.

Mr. Moffat was sincerely anxious to get my approval of this statement, and I was astonished when Mike MacDermot, the Press Information Secretary, came in to add a few words to the answer which considerably strengthened it. The eagerness which these State Department officials showed in correcting the President's original phrasing convinced me that the President had acted in the first instance without consulting the State

Department and, indeed, Roosevelt himself confirmed this a few weeks later. I had gone in to see him about some other matter—it was easy enough to see him before he became really mad at us—and he referred to this incident. He said in effect:

"It was really an oversight of mine. I was sitting in my office here one Sunday night and I was looking at the map there, and thinking of what Hitler had been saying about encirclement. I thought what a great thing it would be to get him to guarantee that he would not attack the various countries surrounding him and then I would get those countries to give a guarantee they would not attack him. So I looked again at the map and I decided to send him a message asking him not to attack various countries around Germany, starting with Latvia, Lithuania and Estonia and so on. When I came to the British Isles, I said Great Britain and Ireland without thinking. Having got the idea I called in a stenographer and sent off the message right away."

In his book, Cordell Hull gives a different version. He said that the President's message was written days before it was sent, that it was carefully drawn up by the President with his White House advisers and sent to him (Mr. Hull) for revision. Hull suggested some alterations, but the President rejected them.

From my subsequent experience with the President I am inclined to believe Mr. Hull's version, but I think that the view I expressed at the time was also correct, and that was that Mr. Hull had not seen the final form of the message before it was dispatched. That was why he was not at all sorry to call attention to President's gaffe in bracketing Great Britain and Ireland.

William Allen White, the Kansas newspaperman who had a national reputation, organised a movement the purpose of which was to mobilise support for President Roosevelt's foreign policy. The movement gained rapid support, particularly in the eastern states, and after some time it was decided to organise the various racial groups in the U.S. to further its objects. Of course it should happen that one of the first of such groups to be so organised was the Irish. The Irish group in Washington was headed by Rossa Downing, a friend of mine, a man who had given good service to Ireland in the past. When I saw in the newspapers the first report of a meeting of this group, I sought out Rossa. He told me that the newspaper reports that the object of the movement was to bring pressure to bear on Ireland to enter the war on England's side were entirely wrong. He said he would make it clear at the next meeting that the last thing they wanted was to get Ireland into the war. In point of fact at the next meeting he warned both the British and the Germans to keep hands off Ireland.

Meanwhile, however, the movement had spread to other cities. The reports I had from Boston were that organisers of the movement there said they were going to bring pressure to bear on de Valera to bring Ireland in on England's side.

Against this there were other Irish groups who said that as a protest against this movement they were going to organise a campaign aimed at preventing America from taking the chestnuts out of the fire for John Bull.

After a few weeks, it seemed to me that the situation was becoming dangerous. In the first place, if the joint campaigns were to continue, the Irish would be split, and I would be deprived of the only weapon I had to save Ireland in the course of the administration's headlong race to save Britain. In the second place, it was clear that the U.S. population as a whole was going overboard in its antagonism to Nazism and if the traditional anti-British attitude of the Irish was to raise its head again, so much the worse for the Irish.

Dublin was as much concerned over all this as I was, but there did not seem to be any solution until one day I had a brainwave. I decided to enlist the support of the British Ambassador. Sir Ronald Lindsay had resigned and was succeeded by Lord Lothian. The latter was a big and breezy bachelor who got along famously with everyone. He was a frequent visitor at our house and my wife still recalls with glee an encounter between him and Sarah Allgood when the discussion had nothing at all to do with politics but whether John M. Synge or Sean O'Casey was the greater playwright.

Anyhow, I went to see Lord Lothian. He listened patiently while I told him of the activities of William Allen White and of the various racial groups he had formed.

"Now," I said, "last week one of the organisers of the Irish group in this William Allen White organisation called on an old friend of mine in Boston and told him that he was going to form a committee in Boston to bring pressure to bear on de Valera to compel him to aid the British war effort. This old man was a Fenian," I continued, "and he threw the organiser out of the house and he said he had up to this time taken no part. But now he was going to see that they would again picket the British Embassy in Washington, as they had done before. You know, of course," I added, "what happened in the First World War."

"My God, this is terrible," said the Ambassador. "What are we to do?"

"Call off the dogs," I said. "You know William Allen White. Give him a ring and tell him to call the whole thing off."

"I can't ring him," he said. "I don't know him that well. I tell you what I will do. I'll get one of our men to call on him in the morning. You may be sure that there will be no more trouble such as your friend had in Boston."

He was as good as his word. Within a week all the activities of the William Allen White organisation ceased so far as the Irish were concerned.

Before I left Lord Lothian, however, I had another word to say:

"It would ease the situation a great deal," I said, "if you would issue a statement to the effect that the British have no intention of invading Ireland."

"Of course we have no such intention," he said.

"Why not issue a statement to that effect?"

"I would be glad to do so, but I have no authority to do it."

"Why not get the authority? Such a statement would make your job and mine much easier. Why not ask them to let you make such a statement?"

"I'll do that," he said.

And, right enough, a few days later, Father Maurice Sheehy of the Catholic University told me that on calling at the Embassy, Lord Lothian had shown him a copy of the telegram he had sent. The Ambassador had asked permission to issue a public statement to the effect that the British had no intention of invading Ireland.

I do not know what answer he got or whether he got any. I do know that such a request to London from the British Ambassador in Washington must have had some effect.

Beyond the usual petty annoyances of being sent from Billy to Jack in my endeavour to get arms to strengthen our defences so as to discourage a possible invader, there was no serious trouble after the war started until November 1940, when the Jervis Bay affair was discussed in the British House of Commons. In trying to explain why a convoy of 42 ships were required to cross the Atlantic with very inadequate protection, Churchill made his first public reference to the Irish ports. He said that the British in trying to keep the sea lines free, while denied the use of the Irish ports, were bearing a burden too heavy for their shoulders, "broad though they be".

I had a cable from Dublin telling me that I was to do my best to head off an American pronouncement which would favour Churchill's view. I saw the Under-Secretary of State, Sumner Welles, and pointed out to him that the ports referred to by Churchill—Cobh, Berehaven, and Lough Swilly—had been handed back to Ireland long after it had been made clear that in the event of war Ireland would remain neutral. The British government before they entered the war was quite aware of the fact that a neutral Ireland could not allow them to use those ports. I said that such a use of our ports by the British would be a violation of our neutrality, which was the policy supported by 99 per cent of our people. Furthermore, if any Irish administration would be mad enough to allow the British to use the ports, we would have a civil war on our hands.

Mr. Welles said that the American administration realised the difficult position we were in, but, at the same time, he had to point out that by a continuation of its present policy of denying the use of the ports to Britain the Irish government was jeopardising its own security. What would be the position, he asked, if Britain were defeated by Germany, who thereafter would dominate both Britain and Ireland? Where then would there be any freedom or democracy for the Irish people? I said that that was a contingency we had to take into account, but there was no element of doubt about the outcome if we took the alternative course. Apart from the fact that our people would be disastrously divided, a departure from our declared policy of neutrality would bring about the immediate destruction of our cities and towns by aerial bombardment for which we were totally unprepared, having no defensive airplanes or anti-aircraft artillery. All our requests for such defences had been denied. I asked him to be assured that there would be no departure from our strict policy of neutrality.

In conclusion, Mr. Welles said that I had made the position of the Irish government clear and he had stated as clearly as he could the American position. The decision rested with the Irish government. There would be no pronouncement from the American government.

As I have said, I kept no diary and I have not had access to any official documents in the Department of External Affairs. I did not ask for such because I thought my request would be turned down. The American government, however, published in June 1958 *Volume III of the Diplomatic Papers 1940* dealing with the foreign relations of the U.S. This volume contains a selection of the communications which passed between the Irish and American governments during the period I am dealing with. To this publication I am indebted for the following memorandum which I handed to Mr. Sumner Welles on the occasion of this interview, which took place on 9 November 1940.

The Irish Legation to the Department of State:

At the outbreak of the war the Irish government in accordance with previously stated policy declared Ireland's neutrality. This policy was supported by all parties in the Dáil and by the entire press of the country.

Britain did not question Ireland's right to declare this policy and no attempt was made to interfere with it. The policy of neutrality has been scrupulously observed. The government established a costly coast-watching service to see that none of the warring powers should take advantage of it. In order to defend Ireland's independence and safeguard its neutrality, the government raised the armed services to

200,000 men, all volunteers. A similar force in the United States in proportion to population would be eight million men.

The friendly feeling between the British and Irish people which had arisen after the settlement of 1938 was steadily increasing, in spite of the fact that the last remaining grievance of the Irish people, that of Partition, had not been remedied.

On November 5th the British Prime Minister in the course of a speech in the House of Commons said that Britain's deprivation of the use of Irish ports as naval and air bases was a serious handicap in fighting the war being waged on British shipping. This was followed by a chorus of demands in the British Parliament and in the British press for the return of those ports to England and this campaign found an echo in the American press. Press statements emanating from London asserted that the good offices of the President of the United States might be enlisted to induce the Irish Government to concede the use of the ports by Britain.

In the view of the Irish Government cession or lease of the ports would be a breach of neutrality which would bring Ireland into the war contrary to the declared policy of the Government and the wishes of 99 per cent of the people.

Mr. de Valera asserted on the 7th of November that Ireland would resist by force any attempt to occupy the port or to impair Ireland's sovereignty by any of the belligerents. That is the determination of the Government and of the people. Under no circumstances will this policy be departed from.

The Government and people of Ireland are in hopes that America, the cradle and home of democracy, will realise the justice of Ireland's attitude in thus seeking to preserve its independence, its peace and its democratic institutions.

I reported this interview to Dublin and a few days later I got a despatch from Dublin which gave a far different version of what Sumner Welles had said to me. According to this, what he had said to me in effect was that since the ports were vital to Britain, we should allow the British to use them, that in any case the U.S. was going to get into the war in the near future, and that then the ports would have to be made available to America, so there was no reason why the Irish should not allow the British access to them immediately.

I was flaming mad when I went down to the State Department to face Sumner Welles with this. A friend of mine in the Department who encountered me in the corridor strongly advised me not to pursue the matter with the Under-Secretary at that time. He said that what had probably happened was that when Welles reported to F.D.R. on the interview, the latter said, "I hope you told Brennan that the British should be given the use of the ports" and Welles realised that if he had correctly interpreted the mind of the President, he would have said just that. My friend advised me to let the matter lie. "If you see him now," he said, "you and he will have a row and thereafter it will be difficult for you two to meet. In any case," he went on, "you have headed off any pronouncement on the matter if such were intended." I decided to take his advice, but during the following night—a sleepless one—I changed my mind. I had always found Sumner Welles a straightforward man, a kindly and courteous gentleman who would never dream of saying one thing to me and something else to his mouthpiece in Dublin. So next day I went to the State Department again. And I was right. Here is Mr. Welles's own account of our interview as recorded in *House Document No. 472 Volume III Foreign Relations of the U.S. Diplomatic Papers 1940*:

December 9, 1940

The Irish Minister called to see me at his request. He stated that he had been advised by his government of a recent conversation which Mr. Gray had had with Prime Minister de Valera by instructions of the Department. In this conversation Mr. Gray was alleged to have said to the Prime Minister that in the last conversation which the Minister and I had had, I had indicated to the Minister that the United States was going to get into the war in the near future and that in such event the naval bases in Éire which the British desire to use would have to be made available to the United States anyway and that, consequently, there was no reason why the Irish government should not make these bases available at once to the British. The Minister said that to the best of his recollections no references of this character had been made in our conversation and he was consequently at a loss to know on what grounds Mr. Gray's conversation is based.

I replied that the Minister was entirely accurate in his recollection and that no such remarks had been made by me, directly or indirectly, nor, for that matter, did such remarks represent the policy of this Government. I stated that I felt sure there was some misunderstanding which could readily be clarified (p. 173).

As to the *Jervis Bay* affair, this is what happened. On 5 November 1940, a convoy of ships bound from Halifax to Britain was intercepted in the Atlantic, some 1400 miles from the coast of the American continent and 600 miles from their destination. There were 42 ships in the convoy and their only defence was one armed merchantman, the *Jervis Bay*, which carried three six-inch guns and which was commanded by Fogarty Fagan, a Tipperary man. The commodore's ship was the *Cornish City*, and as the commodore was ill, the captain of the *Cornish City* had to take charge. When the German cruiser, the *Scharnhorst*, appeared, it looked as if the convoy would be utterly lost, but Fogarty Fagan radioed to the acting commodore that he was going to attack the German cruiser to enable the ships to get away. Orders were given to the ships to scatter to the west and north. Fogarty Fagan steamed right into the German's guns, which raked his ship from stem to stern. His right arm was shot off, but he held on to the riggings with his left hand, still ordering full steam ahead. His ship was literally blown out of the water. He saved the convoy at the expense of his life and that of every member of his crew. Only five of the 42 ships were sunk and all the others found safe port. The captain of the *Cornish City* who substituted for the commodore was none other than Captain Jack O'Neill, now joint general manager of Irish Shipping.

As for Churchill's flimsy pretext that the near disaster was due to the nonavailability of the Irish ports, it was perfectly true, as I told Sumner Welles, that after Dunkirk any ships approaching Britain had to use the northern route. Of course Churchill knew this very well, but he could not resist the opportunity of making the Irish the scapegoat for the British shortcomings.

The British were persistent, however. Hull reveals (p. 872) that when Lord Lothian, the British Ambassador, saw him after a visit to England he said that:

"The first consideration was to secure permission to occupy Irish harbours. Undoubtedly he would like to have our diplomatic assistance—", but I interrupted him by saying:

"In my opinion, de Valera and his associates will not agree to anything at the present. Any aid from us therefore seems virtually impossible just now."

So at that point our protests seemed to be having some effect. Of course, at the time, I had no means of knowing of those exchanges between the British and American governments, but I did know that the British and the Anglophiles in America were straining every nerve to get Ireland into the war by hook or by crook, not so much because of any real contribution Ireland could have made towards the war effort, but because the moral line-up could not be considered complete if the Irish held aloof.

Cordell Hull in his book quotes a letter which Churchill sent to Roosevelt on 7 December 1940. In it he said that there were four ways in which the U.S. could help England. The first three do not concern us here. The fourth was that the U.S. should use her influence in getting naval and air stations in Éire for Britain. The British Prime Minister said:

> If it were proclaimed an American interest that the resistance of Great Britain should be prolonged and the Atlantic route kept open for the important armaments now being prepared for Great Britain in North America, *the Irish in the U.S. might be willing to point out to the Government of Éire the dangers which its present policy was creating for the U.S. itself.*

In the same letter Churchill held out a bait which was calculated to appeal to the Irish in the U.S. as well as at home. He said, "I do not doubt that if the government of Éire would show its solidarity with the democracies of the English-speaking world at this crisis, a Council of Defence of all Ireland could be set up out of which the unity of the island would probably in some form or other emerge after the war."

Several times in talks with State Department officials suggestions of an arrangement along those lines were informally thrown out to me, without however disclosing that the original idea was Churchill's. My reply, of course, was that we had the right to the unity of Ireland and we had the right to remain neutral, and it was ridiculous to suggest that we should abandon one right as the price to be paid for being conceded the other. In any case we were not interested in any promises as to what would happen after the war. We had had our fill of promises unfulfilled after the First World War.

Cordell Hull, in his book, says:

> During the period of the European war, Éire benefited by the program of the American government and people to aid the British Commonwealth as a whole. After the fall of France we made available 20,000 rifles to the Irish Army (p. 1351).

I have no doubt at all but that Mr. Hull believed this to be true. Actually it is not. The rifles certainly came from the U.S., but they were not made available to us by the U.S. government. What happened was that following my instructions, I was besieging various departments for arms. The State Department could do nothing and neither could the Treasury, or the Army, or the Navy. In the State Department I was bluntly told that any arms the U.S. had to spare were to go to the belligerents who were actually fighting against the Nazi tyranny. One day the Secretary of the Treasury, Henry Morgenthau, Junior, said to me that owing to a directive he could not sell the arms to us since we were not a belligerent, but he could sell them to, say, Canada, and the Canadians could let us have our share. He said I should see Captain Mac Blank.

I saw Captain Mac Blank that very day and learned, to my surprise, that he had on hand some 250,000 rifles which he could dispose of. They were all in good condition though some of them had been used. My surprise was due to the fact that the British had been clamouring for such material ever since Dunkirk without very much success. I decided at once to cut out the roundabout approach suggested by Morgenthau, so I went to the Willard Hotel in which were located the offices of the British Purchasing Commission, headed by Mr. Arthur B. Purvis, a Canadian. While I waited to see him, I was amused to notice that his windows on the tenth floor of the hotel were protected by barbed wire.

When Mr. Purvis came in, he was accompanied by Lord Thingumy, who as I knew from my reading of the morning papers had made a speech in New York the night before. I congratulated the noble lord on his speech, which I had not read, and said it was grand, it was perfect, it was what was wanted. The noble lord was delighted with me, and this paved the way for my talk with Mr. Purvis. I told the latter that I knew where 250,000 rifles were to be had with adequate ammunition. He almost turned pale.

"Where are they?" he asked.

"I am not going to tell you," I said, "until you give me your word that I will get my share of them."

"You can't get them," he said, "there is a directive which—"

"All right," I said. "Let us forget about them."

"Wait, wait," he said. "I'll arrange that you get—you say there are 250,000—I'll arrange that you get 20,000 rifles and ammunition for them. How about it?"

I asked him if he were completely satisfied that he could make his promise good. Maybe the British government might have different ideas.

"Look," he said, "we are desperately in need of these small arms. I'm sure they will agree to any arrangement I shall make. But let us make doubly sure. Suppose we go to see the Ambassador. You would take his assurances?"

I said I would, so we belted off to the Embassy, where Lord Lothian readily agreed to the arrangement. I then told them where the rifles were. I had, of course, reported all this to Dublin and several weeks later I had a wire from Dublin asking what the position was. The rifles had not arrived and there was no word of them. I saw Lord Lothian immediately and, luckily, found that Mr. Purvis was with him. I told them that Dublin was getting anxious about the rifles. Lord Lothian looked at Purvis.

"Shall we tell him?" he asked.

"You'd better," said Purvis.

"Well," said the Ambassador, "the fact is that the rifles are on the high seas in a boat which should arrive in Liverpool early next week. I want you to make sure that your people will be there to take your share when the boat arrives."

He added with a grin:

"I'd hate to think that you were in a position to say that the British broke their word."

"You're not thinking of the Treaty of Limerick by any chance?" I said.

That was how we got the rifles. I have no doubt that Lord Lothian told Mr. Hull of the arrangement that had been made.

Here, I might mention the fact that in the various controversies with the U.S. government, before and during the war, I had no trouble at all with the British. On the day my predecessor, Michael MacWhite, left Washington and I became the Chargé d'Affaires, I had a ring from Sir Ronald Lindsay, the British Ambassador, saying he would like to call on me. I said that protocol ordained that I should call on him first.

"Never mind protocol," he said. "Can I come along?"

He was a tall Scotchman, rather shy and awkward, and it was said he was a difficult man to talk to, but when he came along we had half an hour's chat with no difficulty whatever. I returned his call and when I was leaving he said he hoped we would see a good deal of each other. I said, why not?

"You don't mind, do you?" he asked.

"Why should I?"

"Well," he said, "I had been given to understand that you were something of an extremist."

"That's funny," I said. "I had had the idea that you were the extremist."

"What do you mean?" he asked.

"Well," I said, "Look at it this way. We want to rule only our own little island, while you claim to rule practically the whole world. Now who is the extremist?"

He laughed gaily, and there we were off on a friendly footing which continued all through his regime and those of his successors Lord Lothian, Lord Halifax and Lord Inverchapel.

A couple of months after his first visit, Sir Ronald Lindsay came to see me again. He said that there were some British battleships in the [Chesapeake] Bay. I told him I had read about them in the papers.

"Well," he said, "the admiral will think it necessary to call on you."

"And that involves something?" I asked.

"Yes. If he calls on you, you will be expected to visit his ship, where you will be received with rolling drums and blaring trumpets. You wouldn't like that."

"I certainly would not," I said.

"I thought so," he said. "Suppose we fix it with an exchange of cards. How about it?"

"That will suit me fine," I said.

A few months later there occurred the occasion in connection with the King's visit in which I was able to save him some embarrassment.

Mr. Hull says:

> I wrote to the President on May 21st 1940, informing him of a telegram I had received three days before from our minister in Dublin, David Gray, an uncle of Mrs. Roosevelt. Irish Prime Minister Eamon de Valera had enquired whether the U.S. government could proclaim the Irish status quo vital to American interests in view of Éire's strategic position commanding Atlantic air and sea traffic. Mr. de Valera thought such a statement would greatly strengthen his leadership in the face of a difficult and uncertain situation in Ireland (p. 1351).

Of course I had no means of knowing the contents of David Gray's communications to the State Department, but I do know that de Valera had asked for such a statement from the American government, not because it would greatly strengthen his leadership but because it might deter the Germans from invading Ireland if they had any thought of doing so and also make the British pause if they had any thought of occupying Ireland on the pretext that they were taking precautions against a possible German invasion.

After Churchill's reference to the Irish ports there began to appear in the American newspapers dispatches, mostly from American special correspondents in Ireland, which were loaded with charges against Ireland and which questioned the sincerity of her leaders in their policy of neutrality. These charges grew and grew and were repeated again and again all through the war years. In some quarters they continued even after the war ended, and this in spite of the evidence that they were false. It was said that Ireland was a hotbed of German spies directed from the German Legation in Dublin whose personnel had been increased a hundredfold after the war started; that German submarines were being refuelled in the Irish ports for their missions in sinking British and American ships; that the Irish people were not allowed to judge the moral issues involved in the war because of the press censorship. The attitude of the Irish government, these dispatches stated, was due entirely to hatred of England. Of course, after Pearl Harbour when America entered the war, this pernicious material increased very considerably.

It was clear to me from the start that all this hostile propaganda came from one source in Dublin. I told Iveagh House that I could end it by having the persons responsible transferred somewhere else. I certainly could have done so, but the authorities at home seemed to think that such a step would be unwise. Now some seventeen or eighteen years later I still think that my advice should have been taken.

As it was not, I had to encounter all this adverse propaganda. I did it as well as I could by giving press interviews, writing to the papers in which such reports appeared, calling on the editors of the newspapers and magazines in Washington, New York, Boston, Chicago, and in whatever other cities I happened to visit, but in all I could do I could not stop the tide. Of course there are thousands of publications in the U.S., and it was often the case that an item which contained a half truth or a whole lie about Ireland which I had contradicted in the case of a Washington or New York paper would appear in twenty or thirty small papers throughout the country weeks or months later. I did succeed, however, in modifying the attitude of most of the Washington and New York dailies, and I got great assistance from Joe Connolly, the General Manager of the Hearst organisation, which included the International News Service. On several occasions he asked me to write a signed article setting out the true position in Ireland and this was published in full in the Hearst press. Generally speaking, the most influential newspaper in the States, the *New York Times*, was very fair, but on one occasion the magazine section of the *New York Sunday Times* had a front page article by the historian Henry Steele Commager, the historian, containing all the old charges which I had refuted many times. I wrote a letter in reply to this and brought it myself to Mr. James, who was then, I think, the Managing Editor. He took me around to the Editor of the Sunday Edition who, when he read the letter, said that it would have little effect because as a letter it would appear only on a back page. He suggested I should reply to Commager in a signed article to which he would give the same prominence as he had given to Commager's article. The article I wrote duly appeared on the front page of the Magazine Section and the Editor sent me a cheque for a hundred dollars, which I returned to him with the request that it be handed over to the Red Cross.

[On another occasion] I went to Geoffrey Parsons, the Editor of the *New York Herald Tribune*, to complain of something which had appeared in his paper. He asked me to come back the next day to see a few people in his organisation. He had there to meet me a dozen members of his editorial staff to discuss Ireland. Our discussion lasted for over two hours, after which they one and all declared that I had answered their questions fairly and fully.

Of course, as I told them, and as I said frequently to the reporters who interviewed me, we had nothing to conceal and they could ask me any questions they wished. The editors and reporters liked this frankness, and I found that invariably they were fair. Even those who had previously written or published something which put Ireland in a bad light were willing to say, having heard me, that if they had known the true position, they would not have done so. This applies to the Americans in general. They are apt to go off at half cock and to "swing wide", as they say themselves, on what they hear or read on something which affects their interests or arouses their emotions. They are generous in the fact that when they are convinced that they have reached their conclusions on false premises, they at once admit their fault. They say, "I didn't know it was like that. I won't make the same mistake the next time."

It was thus in the case of all the Americans I met, but there are an awful lot of them, and of course I could not get around to them all. Indeed, my small efforts to offset the venomous propaganda against us seemed hopeless at times. But in this propaganda battle I got valuable assistance, not only from supposedly pro-British American organs, but from totally unexpected quarters such as the pro-British *Irish Times*, the London *Times*, and from the official reports of the House of Lords.

An editorial which appeared in *The Irish Times* on 6 November 1940 I quoted often. It bears so much on many of the questions raised that I must quote it in full. It was headed "Dangerous Talk", and it said:

We deprecate the loose talk concerning Ireland which occasionally creeps into the proceedings of the British Parliament. Yesterday the Prime Minister of England, Mr. Winston Churchill, commented upon "the recent recrudescence of U-boat sinkings in the Atlantic approaches" to Great Britain. He deplored as "a most heavy and grievous burden" the fact that his country was not at liberty to use the South and West coasts of Ireland for the refuelling of flotillas and aircraft; and, in so speaking, Mr. Churchill committed no breach of propriety. We wish that other speakers to the debate had paid equal respect to propriety. A Labour member, Mr. Lees Smith, declared that "Germany now had ports west of theirs (Great Britain's), and those ports were on the West coast of Ireland"; while a Mr. Tinker—also a Labour member—announced, with magnificent ambiguity, that "the position regarding the west coast of Ireland was deplorable". The British Parliament has a reputation for fairness, and this sort of talk does no credit to it. Mr. de Valera's Government has proclaimed the country's neutrality, and has shown no reason, so far as we are aware, why the sincerity of that proclamation should be held in doubt. Concerning the issues at stake in the European war, the opinions of Irishmen differ and, under a democratic regime, are at liberty to differ: but the people have endorsed their government's policy, and are prepared to abide by it. Two years ago Mr. de Valera gave an assurance that the territory of the State would not be used by any Power as a base for attack upon any other. We are satisfied that the promise has been kept. We are satisfied that all this talk about the refuelling of belligerent submarines from depots on the Irish coast is so much moonshine. In the first place, the people do not wish to be embroiled in the European war and are disinclined to run any risk that may embroil them in it. In the second place, it is extremely doubtful whether any such operation as the refuelling of submarines could be undertaken without discovery. Since the establishment of the Local Security Force, Ireland has been better policed than at any previous time in her history; and this new force—the eyes and ears of the Army, in Mr. de Valera's phrase—is consecrated to one cause, and to one cause only—the defence of Irish neutrality.

In justice to the British government, we think that it pays little attention to the whirling words of parliamentary backbenchers. A fortnight ago Lord Snell administered a snub to the Reverend Dr. Little, Unionist member for Co. Down, who had alleged that German submarines were being supplied from the territory of the twenty-six counties. The British Government, said Lord Snell, had no evidence that there was any truth in these allegations. In view of our own Government's professed policy, members of parliament would be well advised to avoid random accusations which are bound to do more harm than good. They are at liberty, like Mr. Churchill, to regret what they please. Great Britain, of her own free will, returned the "Treaty Ports" into Irish custody. If the exigencies of war have given her any cause to regret that action, any of her citizens is at liberty to say so. It is quite another thing to prefer mischievous and unsubstantiated charges against a nation and Government which have made their attitude clear beyond doubt.

With regard to the size and influence of the German Legation in Dublin, here is another quotation I was able to use. It is from the London *Times* of 17 July 1940.

Many wild statements have been made in Great Britain about the size and influence of the German Legation in Dublin. Actually it has not more than half a dozen men with two or three women typists. Its behaviour has been uniformly correct, and the stories of its activities as a vast centre of espionage are without foundation.

In March 1942 a Dublin dispatch to the American Magazine *Fortune* stated:

It has been stated that German Diplomatic Representation in Éire exceeds 2,000. Actually there are nothing like that many Germans in Éire all told. . . . German diplomatic representation in Éire stands at the previous figure of five with a staff of one janitor and three typists, and there are fewer than 400 Germans in the whole country.

James Welland, the Staff Correspondent of the *Chicago Sunday Times*, reported to his paper on 11 October 1942 on the charge that the German Legation in Dublin was a listening post from which information regarding movements of British and American forces was transmitted to Germany. He said that there would be no difficulty in picking up such information and transmitting it to the German Legation in Dublin, but he asked how they could convey the information to Germany. They were not in telephonic communication with the continent, and they could not use the short wave transmitters without the authorities, both Irish and British, knowing it. He added: "It would not take the British long to protest if they picked up radio messages emanating from Dublin, and there have been no such protests."

The charge that German submarines were being refuelled in Irish ports was vigorously denied by de Valera. The matter was debated in the British House of Lords, where Lord Strabolgi pointed out that it would be impossible for such refuelling to occur without its being observed, and Lord Snell, replying for the government, labelled such reports as "imaginings" and stated specifically that the government had no evidence to the effect that enemy submarines were being supplied from the Irish territory.

If there had been such refuelling, it was the business of the British to see that it was stopped. The British at the time had a naval attaché attached to the British Diplomatic office in Dublin and, of course, he had his agents in every port in Ireland to keep him informed of all activities around the Irish coast.

The *New York Times* on 10 November 1940 published a dispatch from Dublin, from which the following is a passage:

Six years ago, before Britain had even considered the question of vacating the occupied ports of Cobh, Berehaven and Lough Swilly, Mr. de Valera, in an interview published in the United States, emphasised that he would be strongly opposed to involving this country in any European war, but he declared that he would utilise all the resources of the State to frustrate any attempt to use Irish territory as a base of attack against Britain. That is the policy Mr. de Valera is pursuing today with the support of a united country. It is recalled here now that former Prime Minister Neville Chamberlain's administration in London handed back the ports to Ireland under the agreement of April 1938, well aware of what the Irish Government's attitude would be in the event of war. Mr. Churchill, who strongly opposed the Agreement, told the House of Commons then that Ireland would be neutral in a war, but the Commons ratified the Agreement, as also did the Irish people in a subsequent general election.

The Dublin correspondent of the *New York Times*, writing on 4 January 1941, said:

Ireland today is as much determined to adhere to her policy of neutrality as she was when the war broke out some sixteen months ago. On this one issue there is complete unanimity amongst all political parties. Even those belonging to the old pro-British Unionist classes feel that no government here could take the risk of leading into war a country so indifferently equipped to meet assaults from the air. To them it is not a question of pro-this or anti-that but the vital question of self-preservation as a nation. This small state of 3,000,000 persons has neither the resources nor the equipment to influence the conflict one way or another. The only thing Ireland possesses of value to either belligerent is her territory, more particularly the sea and air bases in the south and west; but to put these at the disposal of one belligerent would be to abandon neutrality and invite immediate assault from the other side. Ireland is determined today to maintain her middle of the road policy and treat as an enemy any invader who tries to gain a foothold here or to seize her ports. Since the outbreak of the war she has meticulously avoided doing anything that would assist one belligerent against the other, and this policy is being rigidly adhered to.

All of these quotations, as I say, I used very freely. But on the question of German espionage—the one which persisted and which was doing us most damage in the U.S.—I was stumped. The fact that parachutists who were German agents had been dropped in Ireland was well known and well publicised. Every one of them had been captured and interned within a few hours of landing. But there was one who had been in the country for some eighteen months before he was captured—a German officer named von Goerz. The explanation which was given to me subsequently was that the Irish Intelligence Service knew very well about this man and that he was left at large because they wanted to discover his contacts. I still do not know what the truth is. I do know that he gave me many a headache. When he was finally captured and it was disclosed that he had been at large in Ireland for eighteen months, I was asked again and again how many more there were that I did not know about.

When I visited Ireland for a short time in 1942, I learned in a rather roundabout fashion of something I should have been informed of much earlier. Shortly after America entered the war the Irish government, in order to meet the supersensitiveness of the Americans on the question of German spies, and realising that the threat to our continued neutrality came more from the Germans than the Allies, actually made an offer to the U.S. which should have disposed of the whole business if it had been accepted. The offer was that the American government should send half a dozen of their best intelligence officers to sit in with our people who were engaged in this struggle against espionage.

So hush-hush were our own people on all these questions that even I, who should have been the first to know of it, knew nothing about it till I ferreted it out for myself. I know, of course, that the government at the time was walking a tightrope and that a mere whisper of such an arrangement would have set Hitler hopping mad. He would say that this was not according to the rules of strict neutrality, particularly as a request which he had made to the Irish government to be allowed to add two or three people to the personnel of the German Legation in Dublin had been brusquely turned down.

The German request had come very late at night; so late, indeed, that Joe Walsh, the Secretary of the Department of External Affairs, had to be roused from his sleep. He pleaded with the German Ambassador von Hempel to postpone it till the next day. Von Hempel refused to do so and Joe had to root Dev out of bed to tell him that there was an urgent message from der Führer which the German Minister wanted to deliver right away. The time was shortly after the successful German occupation of Holland, Denmark and Norway. In Dev's mind, Hitler's message could mean only invasion. So he rang up Frank Aiken, who straight away alerted the army.

When von Hempel arrived, all he had to ask for was clearance at the airport for two or three more people to augment his staff. Dev said:

"You have all the staff you want here. Why do you want more? After all, you are not doing more business with us than you were doing before."

All that poor von Hempel could say was that the Führer desired it. He said that the new appointees would arrive by plane on the following Saturday.

"All right," said Dev, "if they come I shall have them arrested."

"This is terrible," said the Minister. "What am I to say to my government?"

"Just tell them what I said," was Dev's reply.

In the upshot the new emissaries from Germany did not come.

The offer to the Americans to allow half a dozen of their best men to sit in with the heads of our intelligence service was turned down. The U.S. Legation said it would be ridiculous to have men in false beards running around the country frightening people. This showed clearly that people in the American Legation did not believe their own propaganda. If they believed, as they said they did, that the activities of German spies in Ireland jeopardised the lives of British and American soldiers and sailors, it is obvious that such a step as was proposed would have been very advantageous and would have been accepted at once.

In March 1941 I was instructed to inform the State Department that General Frank Aiken, the Minister for Defence, intended to visit the United States for the purpose of purchasing arms, munitions and ships. The official who received me was very cool indeed.

"We know nothing about this visit," he said.

The attitude of this official whom I met officially for the first time was so glacial and so unlike that of all the other U.S. officials that I suspected that the dice had been loaded against Frank from the very start. I was to receive confirmation of this fact later.

I explained as courteously as I could that the purpose of my call was to tell him of General Aiken's forthcoming visit, and he grudgingly noted this fact. When Frank arrived, I made the usual application for an interview with the President and the Secretary of State and was told that the matter would be arranged as expeditiously as possible but that there might be some delay in the case of the President as he was unusually busy. Meanwhile I was to introduce General Aiken to Mr. Joseph Greene, the State Department official who was the liaison officer between representatives of foreign governments and the armed services. Joe, an old friend of mine, was as usual courteous and kindly. He introduced Frank to the appropriate officers in the Army, Navy and Air Force, and while awaiting the promised interview with the President, Joe arranged for Frank to visit certain airplane factories, air bases, etc., throughout the country. It was understood that as soon as I got word from the White House, Frank's tour would be cut short, and he would return to Washington.

Seventeen days elapsed before Frank rang me up from California. He said he was returning to Washington to say goodbye before returning to Ireland. He had got fed up with the situation. He knew, of course, that I had been pressing the State Department every day about the interview with the President and that every day I had been put off with one excuse or another. He knew, too, that the treatment he was receiving at the hands of the White House was in strange contrast to that accorded to every other Minister of State who visited Washington and particularly to that accorded to Winston Churchill, who had been in Washington a few months before. Roosevelt had met and welcomed the British Prime Minister a hundred miles out in Chesapeake Bay. I saw Sumner Welles next day and told him of Frank's decision. He was genuinely distressed.

"Get him to wait," he said. "Give me a day or two more. This must not be allowed to happen. I may have word for you tomorrow."

And right enough when Frank came back the next day, I was able to tell him that the President would see him on the following day at 11.30 a.m. So there we were at the White House at the appointed time received in the outer room by Colonel Watson, the President's secretary, and conducted almost at once into Franklin D. Roosevelt's office. He was seated at his desk and his greetings for us seemed cordial enough. His technique with any visitor, particularly one who might have awkward questions to ask, was invariably the same. He would talk for twenty minutes, at the end of which time the visitor was supposed to leave. The signal that the interview was over was the entrance of Colonel Watson.

On this occasion F.D.R. surpassed himself. Having listened to Frank for about two minutes, he began to talk and he continued to talk of his great regard for Ireland. He told us all the stories regarding Ireland which he had previously told Sean T. and myself and which indeed I had heard from him many times. I was made aware of the fact that the twenty minutes were up when Colonel Watson wandered in and began to pace up and down the floor.

Frank ignored the interruption. He had not yet got in his say and he was determined to do so. Colonel Watson went out and Frank began to talk. He said that no one could doubt Ireland's attitude towards Fascism. We alone in Europe had actually defeated a threatened Fascist uprising in our own country. We would like to be in a position to meet an invader wherever he might come from, and that was why we needed arms, munitions and ships. We had recruited no fewer than 250,000 in our various forces. They were ready to defend our territory, but they were poorly equipped. The position was complicated by the attitude of the British, whose forces were massed on the unnatural border separating the six counties from the rest of the country. Roosevelt interrupted him.

"Listen, General," he said. "I believe in talking straight. You are reported as having said that it does not matter to Ireland whether England or Germany wins this war."

"When and where am I supposed to have said that?" asked Frank.

I intervened and said:

"Mr. President, I have been present at every interview General Aiken gave, and I assure you he never said anything of the kind."

As if there had been no denial, F.D.R. went on to say that it was stupid folly to say it did not matter if Germany won the war. If that happened, the whole world was in danger of coming under the heel of merciless tyranny in the form of a Nazi dictatorship. The American people in common with the peoples opposing this infamous attempt at world subjugation were very much concerned. F.D.R. himself had gone so far as to have the seas patrolled to within a hundred miles of the American coast to spot the German submarines who were preying on their shipping. He intended to extend this patrol area to a thousand miles.

"There is something you might do," he said. "You might patrol the seas off the west and south coasts of Ireland to spot these same submarines. We could spare you a few planes for that purpose."

Frank said that we had had no trouble from submarines. What we were afraid of was an invasion. He took it that the people of Ireland would have the President's sympathy in case of aggression.

"Yes," said F.D.R., "German aggression."

"Or British aggression," said Frank.

The President became very angry. He said it was preposterous to suggest that the British had any intention of becoming an aggressor in the case of Ireland.

"If that is so," said Frank, "why cannot they say so? We have asked them to—"

The President interrupted him again.

"What you have to fear," he said, "is German aggression."

"Or British aggression," said Frank again.

At this the President gave striking evidence of his indignation. The Negro servants had entered, no doubt urged by Colonel Watson, and had begun to place a tablecloth and some silver on the President's desk, preparatory to serving his lunch. When Frank repeated "British aggression", the President caught a corner of the cloth and jerked it across the table so that some of the silver was hurled across the floor.

"I never heard anything so preposterous in all my life," he cried, jerking his head backwards and forward.

"Wouldn't it be a simple thing for them to give us a guarantee?" said Frank.

"Why, I could give you that guarantee right now," said F.D.R.

"Perhaps, Mr. President," I said, "you could do something along that line. Perhaps you could point out to Mr. Churchill that it would ease the situation very considerably if he would give that guarantee."

"Of course he'd give it," replied the President. "I could get it from him in the morning."

This was a good note on which to end the interview, so we thanked him and withdrew.

Some time during the interview the President had said that he might be able to give us a few ships from amongst those which were immobilised in U.S. ports. Frank later told me that he had no recollection of this. He reminded me that if it had been said, it had made little impression on me because I did not mention it in the report of the interview which I later sent to Dublin I was to remember the comment later, however.

As regards the guarantee, of course we never got it, but I made sure that the President should not be allowed to forget his promise. I saw Sumner Welles and asked him about it. His reply was that this had been a matter between the President and me. He had had nothing to do with it and could not take it up. I asked if he would arrange for me to see the President, and he said he would try to do so.

I never did see F.D.R. again on that particular point. I did, however, enrol the support of our friends in the Senate and House. I told them about the promise of a guarantee from Britain and during the ensuing months, which was quite a critical period, they invariably raised the question with F.D.R. whenever they went to see him on other matters, which was often. He dodged the question again and again, but they were satisfied that the mere reminding him of the matter had a salutary effect.

In his book Mr. Cordell Hull gives an account of his meeting with Frank Aiken. It is fairly full, but not full enough. He does not say that when we entered his office he took me for Frank and Frank for me. He started off by telling me what a splendid minister Mr. Brennan was and how ably he had represented Ireland in Washington during the time he had been in the Irish Legation.

Now I had met Mr. Hull at least a dozen times at various official functions, but he never once recognised me. Worse, most of the heads of missions had the same experience at his hands. Indeed at the annual reception given by the Secretary of State and his wife, a courteous lady who never forgot anyone, Mrs. Hull, standing beside him, had to tell him the names of each diplomat as he came to the reception line. Mr. Hull went along all the time with his head bowed as if he were always in deep thought.

He says in his book:

> In March 1941, the Irish Minister for Defence, General Frank Aiken, arrived in the U.S. with letters of introduction from Mr. de Valera to the President and to me for the purpose of purchasing arms, munitions and ships. In his conversation with leading members of our government, Aiken showed himself to be strongly anti-British.

This was not true. Whatever Frank's feelings were, he had not on the occasion of this visit shown himself strongly anti-British in his conversations with members of the U.S. government, leading or otherwise. What Mr. Hull had in mind was not anything Frank said or did since his arrival in the U.S., but the advices he had had from the American Legation in Dublin, which portrayed not only Frank Aiken but every member of the government, with perhaps one or two exceptions, as anti-British. For instance, following the passage just quoted, Mr. Hull says:

> Minister Gray reported to us from Dublin on April 8th that the Aiken mission was being exploited by the Irish Government to arouse anti-British sentiment and to indicate American approval of Irish policy. He suggested that the time had come for us to adopt a firmer attitude and demand from de Valera a definite clarification of his position.
>
> I agreed. We authorised Gray on April 10th to take up with the Irish Prime Minister certain statements de Valera had broadcast to this country to the effect that Britain was blockading Éire as much as Germany and implying that Britain was fighting an imperialist war rather than defending democratic liberties. We requested Minister Gray to lose no opportunity generally to impress on the Irish, the United States Government's determination and the scope of its effort in carrying out its policy of opposition to the forces of aggression. He was also to emphasise the President's profound belief, which had the backing of public opinion here, that the democratic forces throughout the world would win through to final victory.
>
> The following day, April 11th, Minister of Defence Aiken called on me to present his letter from Mr. de Valera. He proceeded to talk for some minutes about the difficulties between Ireland and Great

Britain for many years, extending down to the present, and about how impossible it was to get Britain to do the proper thing and the like—all of which, I thought, related very little to the realities of the present situation.

My recollection of the interview was that Mr. Hull did not even seem to hear what Frank was saying, and these words prove it. What Frank said was that Ireland had adopted the policy of neutrality and that this policy was supported by all but less than one per cent of her people. We would defend that position against any aggressor, however poorly armed and equipped we were. We had the men, but we did not have the arms, and we wanted them badly. Britain might have helped by giving us a guarantee that she would not attack us, but instead of that, she had massed her troops on our borders, ostensibly to be ready to repel an attack on our territory by the Germans. No one could repel such an attack better than the Irish themselves if they had the arms and equipment. We badly needed these and since the blockade hit us in the matter of bringing in supplies of raw materials for our industries and food and foodstuffs, we wanted to buy some ships to supply the want.

Mr. Hull, as I say, did not seem to hear all this. He was concentrating on his reply. He says:

In reply, I spoke very highly of Ireland and of the interest of the American people in her present and future welfare, but I added: There is another tremendously important angle to the present situation, which is imperatively claiming constant attention and effort on our part—and this relates to the world movement of conquest by force on the part of Berlin and Tokyo. I then made a long exposition of our policy from 1933 on, as we warned again and again . . .

Long exposition was right. The Secretary of State lectured us for nearly an hour about the iniquities of the Germans and Japanese. At the end of his account of the lecture, he adds:

"General Aiken had practically no comment to make."

But Frank had a comment to make to me as we walked away from the State Department. "The poor old man," he said, "why have they left him so long in that post?"

About a week after this interview, John W. McCormack, the majority leader in the House of Representatives, asked me to come and see him. He was in high jinks. The Chief (as he always called Roosevelt, whom he adored) had told him that he had decided to give us two ships to convey much-needed food and supplies to Ireland. Roosevelt was going to make an announcement to this effect on the following day. John knew nothing about the ships except that they were cargo boats of eight or ten thousand tons. I sent off a cable to Dublin announcing the glad news. Frank Aiken, who was still with us, agreed that it showed a change of heart.

A few hours later a sudden thought struck me. I remembered F.D.R.'s vague reference to immobilised ships. I said to Frank:

"As sure as God is in heaven, what he (F.D.R.) has in mind is the interned ships belonging to Germany or Italy."

"He wouldn't do that," said Frank.

"I'm going to make sure," I said, and I rang up John McCormack. I caught him just as he was about to leave his office and he agreed to wait for me. When I entered his office, he asked:

"What's the matter?"

"About those ships the President is giving us. Do you know whether they are German or Italian ships which are interned?"

"What difference would that make?"

"Well, we could not take them, that's all. Our neutrality would be at once jeopardised. Apart from other considerations, if we took them and did not pay the owners for them, we would be in bad with the Germans or the Italians. If we did pay for them, we would be in bad with the British."

"What on earth am I to do?" asked John.

"Why not see the President at once and ask him not to make that announcement? If he makes it, and if we refuse to take the ships, it will be very awkward for all concerned."

Of course John saw the point at once. He rang up the White House and got an immediate appointment. I waited till he came back from the White House.

"You're right," he said. "They are Italian ships. He's not going to make the announcement. He made a mistake."

I did not contradict John, but I was perfectly satisfied in my own mind that there had been no mistake. F.D.R. was shrewd enough to know what the consequences would be if we had accepted those ships. When I got back to the Legation and reported to Frank, he said:

"You may not be a great detective story writer, but that's as good a piece of detection as I have ever known."

Mr. Hull states that on 25 April, two weeks after Frank and I had called on him, he cabled to Minister Gray in Dublin that he should tell de Valera that the Americans sympathised with the fact that the reduction in shipping had brought about a food shortage in Ireland and that the U.S. was willing to negotiate for the transfer of a couple of freighters to transport food from the U.S. to Ireland. Mr. Hull goes on:

"I instructed Gray. . . to say that this government had observed with regret, from General Aiken's conversations with various officials here, that the latter's attitude towards the British appeared to be one of blind hostility. This point of view, I said, seemed to be utterly lacking in any appreciation of the fact, which appeared completely clear to this government, that Ireland's future security and safety inevitably depended on Britain's triumph. I continued that the U.S. Government, as the Irish Prime Minister fully realised, believed that the future security of liberty and democracy in the world rested on an ultimate victory of the British and of the other nations resisting aggression, and that this Government was pledged, in conformity with its declared policy, to do everything practicable to help these nations in their struggle. Any Irish policy that was contrary to this U.S. objective would provide no basis for fruitful and helpful cooperation between Ireland and the U.S. I further requested Gray to state very definitely to Mr. de Valera, that in accordance with our policy we would continue to make available to Britain and the Empire and to other countries resisting aggression, all our production of military and naval material not required for our rearmament programme. We could not therefore make it available to Éire until that Government was ready to show a more cooperative attitude toward the war efforts of those nations. This government, I concluded, did not question the determination of the right of the Irish people to maintain their neutrality, but between a policy of this character and one which potentially, at least, gave real encouragement to Germany, there was a clear distinction.

Mr. Hull adds, "An exchange of notes with the Irish Government followed." Mr. Hull is right in saying an exchange of notes followed, but he does not tell the nature of those notes. I still recall, with pride, the terms of the letter I was instructed to bring to the State Department in answer to Mr. Hull's tirade of 25 April 1941. It deplored the tone and content of the State Department's note. It said that aggression was nothing new to us. We had been facing and fighting it alone for over seven hundred years and we would continue to do so if necessary. The letter went on to say that General Aiken's views were shared by every member of the Irish government. Since the two ships the U.S. government was prepared to give us were offered in such terms, we could not accept them.

As I have said, I have had no access to the official documents in the Department of External Affairs. I regret it in this case, for I would have liked to quote the answer our government made to the U.S. on this occasion. I have given the gist of the answer and I am sure it is correct. Even now, after so many years, I can recall the joy I felt when I called at the State Department and read that proud reply.

The man I saw, however, was not Cordell Hull, but Sumner Welles. He was terribly distressed, and he toyed with the idea of pretending that Mr. Hull's instructions to Gray on 25 April had not been issued and that our reply had not been received, but I showed him that that course was impossible. He said he would try to remedy the damage and, right enough, a few days later the State Department sent a letter to Dublin which contained what was in effect an apology for the harsh tone of the previous communication and practically begged the Irish government to accept the two freighters.

But there were no freighters in the offing at all. Somewhere along the line, F.D.R., stung into action by our friends in the

Senate and House who knew that we were desperately anxious to get hold of a couple of ships, publicly announced that he had decided to make available to the Irish government two ships to bring much needed food and supplies to Ireland. I went immediately to the State Department to ask about those ships. I was told I should see Admiral Emory S. Land, head of the Maritime Commission, later called the War Shipping Administration. Now I knew Jerry Land, as everybody called him, very well, and when I went to see him I expected that he and I would have a quiet talk about the matter. Instead, I found myself confronting twelve stony-faced men ranged around a long table with Jerry Land in the chair. Jerry, without batting an eye, addressed me:

"Maybe you would tell us, Your Excellency, what it is you want?"

"Sure," I said. "We want two freighters."

"What sort of freighters?" asked Jerry.

"I don't know," I said, "except that they should be in the region of eight to ten thousand tons."

"To carry what?"

"Well, whatever freight we wanted or was available—mainly grain, possibly general cargo."

A man down the table said:

"Why can't you use the two freighters which are now tied up in Irish ports?"

"I know nothing about them," I said. "If there are two freighters tied up in Irish ports, there must be some good reason why our government is not using them. Maybe you will tell me why?"

In the subsequent exchange it appeared that the two ships in question were under the Estonian or the Latvian flag, and since these two countries had been overrun by the Russians, the Soviets claimed ownership of them.

"Look," I said to my questioner, "there are a lot of Italian and German ships tied up in American ports, why do you not use them?"

"We can't," he said.

"And why not?" I asked.

"Because we are neutral."

"And have you forgotten," I said, "that Ireland is also neutral?"

He had, of course, no answer to this. I turned to Jerry Land and said, "The only reason I am here, Admiral, is that the President of the United States said he was prepared to make available two ships for Ireland. I thought when I came here that you would have an array of ships from which I could select two."

"That would be all right," said Jerry, "if we had the ships. The President expects me to deal a whole pack when I have only twenty-six cards in my hands."

"All right, Admiral," I said. "The President announced that he was going to give us two ships and you say that you do not have them. It is clear that someone has made a mistake and I must so report to my government."

With that I got up and left the room. Jerry, plainly taken aback, followed me and led me into another room.

"Listen," he said, "I am nearly at my wits' ends. I don't have the ships. That's the honest truth. But the President had committed us in your case, and I will do what I can. Can you get hold of someone who can tell us what sort of ships you want? If you do that, I think I can fix up something."

A few days later I got Joe Brennan, our Consul in Boston, to handle this business. There were tantalising delays. It was found that under existing laws the U.S. government could not sell, lend, or give any ships to us. A bill was introduced in Congress to enable the U.S. government to transfer two U.S. ships to the "Government of the Irish Republic," which of course wasn't then in existence. But that was not the flaw that was found in this bill; it was something else which I cannot recall. It was then considered whether they could be given under Lend Lease, but the lawyers turned this down, too, because Lend Lease applied only to countries at war. Finally some lawyers found that the ships could be chartered to the U.S. Shipping Line and that line could re-charter them to us. It all took a long time, particularly as the two ships decided on, *The West Neris* and *The West Hematite*, had to be repaired and refitted in U.S. dockyards.

At last, however, we got them. The two ships sailed the seven seas as the *Irish Pine* and the *Irish Oak*, flying the Irish flag. They were both sunk, and this was the subject of a further controversy between the two governments.

Frank Aiken and I called on the Archbishop of Baltimore and Washington. Frank was very doubtful as to the outcome of the visit. He knew, as did everyone else, that Archbishop Curley, a native of Athlone and a man of very downright views, had been for years a lively and persistent critic of de Valera. Almost every year he visited Ireland, and on his return he had a new attack to make on the Irish leader. I assured Frank that we would hear nothing of that kind on this occasion. I told him that in 1937, on the eve of a brief visit to Ireland, I realised it might be considered strange that though I had been three years in his Archdiocese, I had never called on him. I consulted Monsignor O'Dwyer of the Catholic University, at that time a great friend of the Archbishop, and we drew up a tactful letter asking for an appointment, which was immediately granted. So Una and I took the train to Baltimore. I warned Una to say nothing at all if the Archbishop should begin to inveigh against de Valera. She said that of course she would say nothing. He opened the door for us himself and led us into a very sparsely furnished sitting-room. There he threw off his skullcap and we exchanged pleasantries until he got on to the subject of de Valera. And what he said would fill a book. Seeing that Una and I were silent, His Grace said:

"Maybe I am talking my head off."

"No," I said. "Of course you are entitled to your views, but a great deal of your information is wrong."

"In what respect?" he asked. "I would be glad to know."

I proceeded, as quietly and as persuasively as I could, to point out the various matters on which he was misinformed. He listened very patiently and when I finished he said with a smile: "Well, maybe you're right. We won't quarrel about it."

On the occasion of the visit of Frank Aiken and myself, I was shocked to see that he had greatly changed. He appeared to be years older than when I had last seen him. We did not have to tell him of the extreme danger Ireland was in, and he said he would do his best to avert it. He suggested that as Sumner Welles was a neighbour of his, he would call on him and impress on him the fact that the neutrality of Ireland should be respected.

He did this, and shortly afterwards there came an opportunity of driving the lesson home. Monsignor Reidy, who at the time was on the staff of the Catholic University and who later became Bishop of Ohio, took advantage of the annual meeting of the American hierarchy in Washington to have the bishops entertain Sumner Welles to dinner. The affair took place in the Shoreham Hotel, and Welles was about the only layman present. The others were all church dignitaries. When the dinner was nearly over, Monsignor Reidy in proposing the toast of honouring their guest adverted to the neutrality of Ireland, a neutrality which must be preserved at all costs because of Ireland's value to the democratic and Christian world. Speaker after speaker followed him, all on the same theme. The American cardinals, archbishops, and bishops left no doubt in Mr. Welles's mind as to how they stood on the question of Ireland's neutrality.

Some time later, Bishop MacCormack, the Rector of the Catholic University, who had not been at the dinner, asked me to come and see him. He said:

"Tell Dev that we are all with him, whatever is said to the contrary. We know that what he decides is best for Ireland, and we will support him to the utmost of our ability. Please tell him that."

Later again, when the clouds became much darker, Martin Conboy, the famous New York lawyer and his secretary, J.C. Walsh, came to Washington and we had a long discussion about what could be done on a nationwide scale to call attention to Ireland's peril, with the idea of rallying the support of all her friends in the U.S. It was decided that on a particular Sunday there should be a Mass offered in some Catholic Church in every city, town, and hamlet throughout the land, for the peace and prosperity of Ireland. This was organised by J.C. Walsh, and, as usual, he did a superb job. I do not recollect what the precise figure was, but on the Sunday selected there were many thousands of Masses for Ireland celebrated throughout the land. Archbishop (later Cardinal) Spellman presided at the Mass of St. Patrick's Cathedral, New York. On the Archbishop's invitation, Leo McCauley, our Consul General in New York, and I occupied special seats in front of the altar. So great was the throng that the vast cathedral was filled, and hundreds were unable to gain admission.

There were only two Catholic bishops who adversely criticised Ireland's stand. I wrote to them both. One of them called on me afterwards to say how sorry he was. He said he had not fully understood the position, and he told me he was going to make amends.

In his book Mr. Hull says:

> In 1941 some hundreds of American technicians and workmen went to Northern Ireland to help the British construct bases there. The Government of Éire asked us in October, and again in November, the purpose of these activities and what the intentions of the American government were. We wrote Irish Minister, Robert Brennan, on November 18, saying that this had been taken up with the President and we were authorised to say that this enquiry related to territory recognised by this Government as part of the United Kingdom and to suggest that the Irish Government address its inquiry to the U.K. government (p. 1354).

This, of course, was the brush-off. It lined up America on the side of Britain in the latter's claim that the Six Counties of North-East Ireland were British territory. That claim was in violent opposition to Wilson's fourteen points and his declaration of self-determination for all nations great and small alike. The Irish people had by a vote of four to one established their claim to possession of the whole island, the boundaries of which were indisputable.

Ireland had been from time immemorial a national entity, so its unnatural division into Southern Ireland, containing twenty-six counties, and Northern Ireland, containing six counties, was a denial of every aim the Americans had in the First World War. We were not slow to point out all this, but the American government was deaf to all our arguments. What mattered was that the war for the principles of freedom was to be won at all costs, even that of trampling underfoot those very principles.

About this time I received instructions to make tentative inquiries as to whether we could obtain a loan of ten million dollars from the U.S. government for the purpose of buying much-needed food and foodstuffs in the U.S. At the State Department I was told to consult Mr. Jesse Jones, who was in charge of several government agencies including the Export-Import Bank. Mr. Jones was a tall and powerfully built Texan who, at the time, was a towering figure in the administration. So far as I know, he had never held any elective post. He had been selected by F.D.R. because of his financial ability and standing as a self-made millionaire. He never made any claim to diplomacy.

I got an appointment with Mr. Jones and arrived at his office at the hour agreed upon. I thought it was a bad augury for my mission when I was kept waiting in an anteroom for the greater part of an hour. When finally I was ushered into his office, Mr. Jones, without a word of apology for my long wait, asked me brusquely what it was I wanted. I realised at once that he had been briefed, but I summoned up all my suavity and politeness and told him the object of my visit.

"You want ten million dollars," he said. "What for?"

"To purchase food and foodstuffs in the U.S."

"How will you get the stuff across to Ireland?"

"In our own ships."

"And who is going to convoy the ships?"

"No one," I replied. "Our ships do not sail in convoy."

"Why not?"

"Because they are safer otherwise."

"You mean that the Germans respect the Irish flag?"

"Well, so far they have done so."

He quite plainly showed his disgust.

"Well, I dunno," he said. "We'll look into the matter, but I don't see that I can give you much encouragement."

I reported this conversation to Dublin and expressed the view that the matter had already been prejudged. I recommended that it should not be further pursued at the time. My recommendation was adopted.

On Sunday 7 December 1941, my wife and I were guests at lunch in the house of Supreme Court Justice William O. Douglas. Amongst the dozen guests was Robert Patterson, the Assistant Secretary for War. Towards the end of the lunch Mr. Patterson was called to the phone. When he rejoined us, he said that the Japanese had attacked Pearl Harbour. He had no details, but he had to get back to his office at once. The luncheon party broke up immediately.

I knew, of course, that henceforth my position representing a neutral country was going to be doubly difficult. Whenever America is at war, the average citizen of the U.S. takes the view that it is a crusade. They are fighting not for any territorial aggrandisement or colonialism. They are simply fighting for right and against wrong. They cannot understand why every right-thinking people is not with them. I knew therefore that in defending the continuing neutrality of our country, I had a hard row to hoe. Besides, I had in mind the mercurial disposition of the Americans, as instanced in the case of Finland. In 1939, shortly after the outbreak of war, Finland had been attacked by Russia. After a gallant fight lasting some three months, she had had to concede a considerable portion of her territory to the invaders. During this period, Mr. Jalmar Procope, the handsome Finnish Minister in Washington, became something like a matinee idol. Whenever there was an event at which diplomats appeared, he was singled out for photographs. His country was lauded to the skies as being the only European country which had paid its World War One debts on the dot. In fact, Mr. Procope was the ideal man and his country was the ideal country.

Yet less than a year later Procope was in the doghouse. The reason was that after Hitler invaded Russia, the Finns thought it a good time to get back their lost territory, so they promptly proceeded to occupy it. Thereafter in American eyes the Finns ceased to be good boys. Gone was the admiration for the Finns, who had uniquely paid their debts; gone was the admiration of a small country fighting for its rights. By taking action against Russia to regain her territory, Finland had put herself on the wrong side, and Mr. Procope, the former matinee idol, was ostracised and finally told to get out. I had all this in mind when on that 7th of December 1941, Una and I drove back to Washington from the residence of Mr. Justice Douglas. I wondered if the fate of Mr. Procope would be ours also. True, we had not engaged in hostilities as the Finns had done, but that was only because of an accident of geography over which neither the Finns nor we had any control. In American eyes non-belligerence in a war in which they are engaged is almost as bad as active hostility.

Here let me say that my fears were unjustified. During the whole period of the war, Una and I never lost a worth-while friend, and it seemed to both of us that people were more than usually kind. Indeed, not once but several times, Mrs. Evelyn McLean, the fabulous Washington hostess who used to entertain over a hundred guests to dinner, went out of her way to place us in the seats of honour at her table, defying Washington protocol inasmuch as many of her guests should have taken precedence over us. Una and I remarked that she invariably did this at a time when Ireland was having a bad press, though she never once adverted to the fact.

Mrs. McLean was the daughter of Tom Walsh, a man who had emigrated from his native Tipperary. He hadn't a penny, but he managed to make his way to the West Coast, where he started prospecting for gold. In the scorching suns of summer and through bitter winters, he persevered for twenty years, and at last he found the gold he sought. He became a multimillionaire overnight, and in Washington he built three enormous mansions. One of them, at the junction of Massachusetts Avenue and Twenty-first Street, his daughter, Mrs. [Evelyn] Walsh McLean, years later presented to the American Red Cross; the second at Tenleytown is now the centre of a new residential estate on the outskirts of the city; the third, Friendship, in the old city of Georgetown, which was a fishing village before the city of Washington was decided on as the capital of the U. S., was still intact at the time Mrs. McLean died a few years ago. It was a vast house on the side of a slope. Behind the house were descending terraces and at the lower level a swimming pool where, in summer, her numerous guests used to relax. Evelyn was the only child of Tom Walsh. She must have been very beautiful, as well as rich, when she first met Ned McLean, the son of the proprietor of the *Washington Post.* They fell head over heels in love. In the ordinary course, since the parents of both were satisfied, they could have had a regular engagement and a subsequent marriage, but they thought it would be more romantic to elope, which they did. She wired to her father from Paris saying they were stony broke, and he wired her ten thousand dollars. Hearing of this, McLean's father, not to be outdone, wired the happy pair another ten thousand. At the end of three months the pair were again stony broke, so they wired for more money, which of course was promptly forthcoming.

The couple returned to Washington, and there came on the scene four or five children, two at least of whom had tragic ends. This was later attributed to the Hope diamond. Somewhere along the line Mrs. McLean had acquired the Hope diamond, which is supposed to bring bad luck to the owner. Evelyn always wore it on a silver chain suspended from her neck, and at least twice I have held it in my hand. I do not know where it is now, but it is certain that something brought bad luck to this lady, who had a very tender heart. She alone braved the U.S. Army when she went down the Mall in Washington to feed the bonus marchers after the First World War. It was she who was the victim of Gaston Means, who said he could recover the Lindbergh baby. She paid this fraud a hundred thousand dollars to recover the baby for the heart-broken parents, not knowing that the child was already dead.

She was all heart and courage. Even at a time when she saw that her own family world was falling to bits, she kept up a brave face. She presided at her dinners with a dignity which would have graced the court of any Queen of France. I was glad to learn that at her deathbed Father Edmund Walsh of Georgetown University, an old friend of hers, was at her side.

On the day after Pearl Harbour, I sat in my place in the diplomatic benches in the House of Representatives and heard F.D.R. denounce the Japanese for their wanton and unprovoked attack on the United States. He labelled 7 December 1941 as "a day of infamy". America was at war.

I got instructions a few days later to deliver a note to the State Department embodying extracts from a speech made by Mr. de Valera expressing Ireland's special sympathy with the U.S. because of their involvement in the war and stating that nevertheless Irish policy would remain unchanged and that Ireland could be only a friendly neutral because of the circumstances of our history and because of the partition of our country.

Mr. Hull, dealing with this note, says:

> At the State Department we had been considering for some days the advisability of a message from the President to Prime Minister de Valera. This seemed to be the appropriate moment to send it. The President agreeing, I dispatched a note to Minister Brennan on December 22nd, attaching the message with which I said I also desired to associate myself. In this the President said in part:
>
> > The policy of the American government now, as in the past, contemplates the hope that all the free institutions, liberties,

and independence which the Irish people now enjoy may be preserved for the full enjoyment of the future. If freedom and liberty are to be preserved, they must now be defended by the human and material resources of all free nations. Your freedom too is at stake. No longer can it be doubted that the policy of Hitler and his Axis associates is the conquest of the entire world and the enslavement of all mankind. I have every confidence that the Irish Government and the Irish people, who love liberty and freedom as dearly as we, will know how to meet their responsibilities in the present situation.

American troops landed in Derry on 26 January 1942, and Dev immediately protested that he had not been consulted by either the British or American governments. He said that this move could have no effect on the Irish people's claim for the union of the whole national territory and for supreme jurisdiction over it. He added that the maintenance of the partition of Ireland was as indefensible as aggressions against small nations elsewhere which in the war it was the avowed purpose of Great Britain and the U.S. to bring to an end.

When Dev's protest was published, the reporters asked F.D.R. what he had to say about it. His reply was:

"Well, that is taking in a lot of territory."

As a matter of fact it was he and not Mr. de Valera who was taking in a lot of territory. After all, Derry was more than three thousand miles from America's shores, and in the view of the old Irish nation, Derry belonged to us and not to the British or the Americans.

Mr. Hull says:

Irish Minister Brennan handed Under-Secretary Welles on February 6th an official text of Mr. de Valera's statement and said that the Irish government and people regarded our landing of troops in Northern Ireland as an official sanction by the U.S. of the partition of Ireland and increasingly believed that these troops were going to be used to attack Irish forces. Welles sought to reassure him.

The President sent further reassurances to Prime Minister de Valera on February 26th. Mr. de Valera thanked the President on April 20th for his assurances and then reiterated his objection to the landing of American troops from the viewpoint of the partition question and asked that Ireland be allowed to purchase necessary military equipment in this country without delay.

The President commented on this in a memorandum to Welles suggesting that no reply be sent and then saying: "If he would only come out of the clouds and quit talking about the quarter of a million Irishmen ready to fight if they had weapons, we would all have higher regard for him. Personally I do not believe there are more than one thousand trained soldiers in the whole of the Free State. Even they are probably efficient only in the use of rifles and shotguns." (p. 1355)

This contemptuous opinion of the Irish fighting forces remained in F.D.R.'s mind. In 1942, when I again pressed my request for arms, he said:

"Yes, I think we could do something. In the beginning of the war we were able to give the farmers in my part of the country nothing but shotguns. Now we have been able to give them rifles. I'm sure that we could be able to give you now a few hundred of those shotguns."

He smiled his old bland smile as he hurled this insult. I felt so humiliated that I did not even report the offer to my government.

Before America was in the war, I had made many speeches in various cities throughout the U.S. in an endeavour to make clear the point of view of our people. I had spoken many times in New York and Washington and occasionally in the cities of New England, the Middle West, and the West Coast. Always I found that the audiences were receptive even when they were not mainly Irish.

After 7 December 1941, however, I tried to dodge as many of such engagements as I could. I realised, of course, that the generous people such as I had found the Americans to be were now concerned not with my grievances, however enormous they appeared in my eyes, but with the likely fate of the husbands, brothers, sweethearts and sons they had sent out to fight in a cause which concerned not merely themselves, but, as they saw it, all humanity.

There were some invitations, however, which were so insistent that I could not refuse them without appearing to be unwilling to face the issue. One of those was from the Nassau Club of Princeton University. Late in 1941 the President of the Club had extracted a promise from me that I would go to Princeton. He reminded me of my promise many times and so finally, in November 1942, I journeyed to Princeton. I was picked up at a small railway station in New Jersey and was being driven to the University before there dawned on me, from the conversation of my host, the realisation that the very word "Nassau" had an Orange connotation. It had not occurred to me before that the Nassau Club might be considered to be the American equivalent of an Orange Lodge, though, of course, that would be a misnomer. I thought of the contents of my speech which I had carefully prepared and decided that I would not alter a line of it.

There were over a hundred people in the hall, the great majority being professors or lecturers in the University. As my address on the occasion was more or less on the lines I delivered at that time in other places, I may be excused if I give the main points I made.

I said that during the past couple of years I had been told many times that it was difficult for the average American to understand Ireland. On the other hand, during a recent visit to Ireland I had found that the Irish were equally puzzled about America. My friends had asked me why on earth American troops had been sent to Northern Ireland. I told them that the object was in the first place to prepare for an invasion of Europe and, in the second place, to defend Ireland from a possible German attack. I had told my Irish friends that the average American considered that those troops should have been welcomed instead of receiving a rebuff in the shape of a vigorous protest by the Irish government. The reply was that an invasion of the continent could have been mounted far more easily from English ports and that as regards the possible invasion by the Germans, the Irish could have looked after themselves far better than any outside force could have done if they had been supplied with the proper equipment. Apart from that, the American authorities should have known that four fifths of the Irish people bitterly resented the partitioning of their country and the U.S. should not have condoned partition by sending U.S. troops to the partitioned areas.

I went on to give a summary of recent Irish history. The Rising of 1916 was the fifth rebellion against British rule in Ireland in 120 years. The Rising was crushed, but a couple of years later the people of all Ireland endorsed the principles of the leaders of the Rising when by four to one they voted in favour of a Republic for all Ireland entirely free from British rule. Acting on this mandate the Irish set up a government to rule the country. The British augmented their already vast forces by recruiting a ruthless and savage force called the Black and Tans, who proceeded to bludgeon the Irish into subjection. The Irish government was driven underground, but it functioned because the Irish people gave their allegiance to it and boycotted the British governmental institutions. The struggle involved a great deal of bloodshed and destruction and lasted for three years. Lloyd George confessed in the British House of Commons that the King's writ no longer ran in Ireland. Urged on by King George, he called for a truce. This resulted in a treaty which was accepted only because the alternative was, in the words of Lloyd George himself, "immediate and terrible war". The British had proposed to throw 300,000 troops into Ireland and conduct a Sherman's march from Antrim to Cork.

I proceeded to give a detailed outline of the treaty which set up two governments in Ireland, one in Dublin embracing twenty-six counties and the other in Belfast governing six counties. The Boundary Commission, which was to have drawn a new boundary between the two sections in accordance with the wishes of the inhabitants, was abortive. The ultra-Tories, who composed the Northern Government, set up a regime which was the very negation of democracy, as indeed partition was in the first instance. I quoted the Hon. Frank Pakenham as saying in the *Daily Telegraph* on 20 January 1938, that the regime in Northern Ireland was of a character which the ordinary Englishman considered to be confined to Central Europe. Frank C. Hannigan stated in *The Progressive*, Madison, Wisconsin, on 30 November 1942, that the Catholic minority in the six north-eastern counties were "ruthlessly oppressed by the Northern Government". Mr. Joseph O'Driscoll, special correspondent of the *New York Herald Tribune*, on 30 January 1938 said that one third of the population of the six counties were virtually debarred from public office. In 1936 a Commission of Enquiry consisting entirely of English people said that the Northern Ireland Executive had taken a position paralleled only by continental dictatorships. Twenty-four distinguished public figures, writers and military leaders had in 1940 stated that the Royal Ulster Constabulary had "incurred the odium attaching to a political police force of the type familiar on the continent of Europe". Amongst the signatories were General Gough, Colonel James Fitzmaurice, the Earl of Antrim, the Duke of St. Albans, the Earl of Ossory and Major General Hugh Montgomery.

I quoted many other sources—none of them Irish Nationalist sources—to show the biased and bigoted character of the Belfast government which had set aside the Habeas Corpus Act and set up a special constabulary force which was recruited exclusively from the Orange Lodges.

I then went on to deal with the new Irish Constitution, which guaranteed freedom of conscience and the free profession and practice of religion. The State built free schools for Catholics, Protestants and Jews alike; it staffed and maintained those schools and it even provided free transportation to bring the children of non-Catholic parents to schools of their choice.

I dealt with the difficulties the Irish authorities were having because of the war. The shortage of gasoline and coal, of raw materials for our industries and so on, and then I went on to deal with our policy of neutrality, which had been the object of attack in certain quarters in America. I said that we had publicly declared in 1932 that in the coming war Ireland would be neutral. This policy had been reaffirmed by the government after the war started. It was backed up by every political party, by the entire metropolitan and provincial press, by the Chambers of Commerce and the Trade Unions and by the leaders of every religious denomination. There had never been such a degree of unanimity shown on any question. It was computed that not fewer than 99 per cent of the people supported the policy of the government. People outside Ireland who did not agree with this policy attributed it to a hatred of Britain, but it was a fact that *The Irish Times*, the leading champion of pro-British feeling in Ireland, was as firm in support of the policy of neutrality as were the ultra-Nationalist newspapers.

We had taken steps to defend our stand by arming our men as well as we could. In the various defence forces we had no fewer than 300,000 men, all volunteers. A similar force in America on the basis of population would number over thirteen million.

I then dealt with the false reports regarding our supposed laxity in dealing with German spies, etc., and concluded:

> The Irish believe they do not have to apologise for or explain their position. They are conscious of their history. From the year A.D. 1000 down to our own time they fought in what seemed a hopeless cause and against terrific odds for the very principles of liberty and justice on which the American nation is founded. Ireland is a small country without great material resources. She is just emerging from a state of subjection which had continued for centuries. At the moment her very existence is at stake. If she is attacked, weak though she is, her sons and daughters will resist to the death, and they will give a good account of themselves. Were she voluntarily to abandon her neutrality now, she would invite civil strife within her borders and annihilation from without. A great country like America with vast resources in manpower and materiel can afford to take great risks because her recovery, whatever the outcome, is inevitable. Not so a small nation; she cannot step in between the Titans and avoid disaster.

American audiences are invariably polite, particularly when listening to non-Americans who have been invited to speak. It is very rarely the case that one hears an interruption or an objection to what the speaker is saying. I did, however, on this occasion expect that there would be some opposition to my remarks, particularly to those I had made about the Orange Order. Not at all. Speaker after speaker rose to thank me for my informative talk. They all said I had thrown a good deal of light on a subject which had had them puzzled.

There followed a great many questions which I answered quite frankly. They were all for the purpose of obtaining further information; there was not one word of adverse criticism of the Irish position. A priest came to me to tell me there were only three or four Catholics in the audience.

It had been arranged that after lunch I was to address a group of ladies, the female members of staff and the wives or daughters of the professors and lecturers. I had been told that there would be thirty or forty present, so I was surprised to find that I had even a larger audience than I had had in the morning. I learned that nearly all the men who had heard me had told their female relatives that they should hear what I had to say. Indeed, the hall was crowded and my talk evoked an even more enthusiastic response than the earlier one. One lady said she had a confession to make. Her people came from Cookstown, County Tyrone. She had had a few words with her husband the night before about the propriety of inviting an Irish Rebel to speak in Nassau Hall, and she had told him quite positively that she would not attend the Ladies' Session. When her husband came back from the morning session, he persuaded her to change her mind. She was very glad she had done so.

The lady turned and addressed me directly:

"Your Excellency," she said, "the great poet Oliver Goldsmith belonged to your people and mine. He wrote a line which now best expresses the way I feel. Of the sermons preached by the old clergymen in the *Deserted Village*, he said: 'And fools who came to scoff, remained to pray.' I frankly confess that this morning I was a fool. I came to scoff. I remain now to pray with you that Ireland may preserve her neutrality and be saved from the holocaust."

The lady's little speech was warmly applauded.

The President of the Club drove me back to the railway station. He said that my address had made many converts.

"There may be some who do not go the whole way with you," he said, "but even they would not now countenance any attempt to force the Irish to abandon their neutrality."

Apart from meetings of various Irish and Catholic organisations which I addressed at this time, there is one that I recall particularly because it gave me a glimpse of the extraordinary subtlety of British propaganda methods. The President of the Calvin Bullock Forum had been urging me for a long time to give a talk to its members, and finally I had to fix a date. It was either towards the end of 1942 or the beginning of 1943.

Snow was falling as I entered No. 1 Wall Street, New York, and was whisked in the elevator up to the top floor. Mr. Bullock received me genially and conducted me through a whole suite of rooms in which were displayed, as in a museum, many exhibits of the Napoleonic era. He explained to me that his grandfather had been an enthusiastic collector of material concerning the Napoleonic wars and his descendants had added to the collection, which was certainly impressive. Mr. Bullock, a stockbroker, as his father and grandfather had been, told me that his father had established the Bullock Forum for the sole purpose of enabling anybody in Wall Street who was interested to keep abreast of foreign affairs by listening to talks by persons who were authorities on such subjects. So every Friday evening after the market had closed, they assembled in the Calvin Bullock Forum to hear such talks.

Mr. Bullock told me that he feared I would have a sparse audience. There had been a serious fall on the market that day and, besides, on account of the snow, many members would have scurried home. So both he and I were really surprised when, on going down to the lower floor and entering the room where my talk was to be given, we had some difficulty in entering, so great was the throng.

"This is a great compliment to you," said my host, and indeed that was the case. We were seated in what seemed to be a little theatre—how any of the small Dublin groups would have coveted it. Beside every seat was a detachable desk which the occupant could use for the purpose of making notes. I delivered my speech and afterwards answered dozens of questions. There was one question to which I had no answer, and it was asked again and again. It was:

"How many Irish are there in the British fighting forces?"

I said quite frankly that I did not know. When the question had been asked for the third time, a tall man who had been unable to get a seat and who stood at the back of the hall, said:

"I can answer that question. The number of Irish in the British fighting forces is not less than 200,000."

Some members of the audience expressed incredulity, but the man said he was in a position to know, and the figure, as he said, was not less than two hundred thousand. I did not know who the man was but, apparently, the audience did, for they readily accepted his answer as being authoritative.

After the meeting the tall man came to me and introduced himself. His name was Wilberforce, and he was, he said, an official of the British Information Service. He introduced another man, whose name I have forgotten, who told me he had some connection with Achill Island. He also was in the same service. I thanked Mr. Wilberforce for coming to my aid while, in my own mind, I was wondering why he had spoken as he did. Surely a man in his position would not have done so without instructions. The question remained in my mind all the way in the train back to Washington. Maybe there were two hundred thousand Irishmen in the British forces, maybe not. I finally decided that whether there were or not, it might be a good card for the British to play in America. It would show that, although the Irish government was not in the war on the side of the Allies, the Irish people were. Maybe, I said to myself, I am not being fair to Mr. Wilberforce. Maybe the British are not so subtle as all that.

In the spring of 1942, as a result of a chance conversation, I learned that a well-known military gentleman, who had an

Irish name—let me call him Major X—was planning a visit to all the American bishops of Irish origin (which meant practically all of them) with a view to getting them to bring all the pressure they could bear on de Valera to change his attitude towards the war. I was given to understand that the project had the blessing of the White House. I immediately took a plane to Boston and saw Cardinal O'Connell. He told me that Major X had not called on him and that if he did so he knew what to say to him. Again he said to me what he had said earlier:

"Tell de Valera to hold fast. Tell him not to budge an inch."

In Philadelphia I called on Cardinal O'Dougherty, who told me that Major X had not called on him. He rather hoped he would do so because he had something to say to him which the Major would not like to hear. It seemed that some years earlier there had been a case in the courts in one of the southern states in the course of which it appeared from the evidence that a priest had divulged some secrets of the confessional. The priest had done nothing of the kind and he offered to give evidence which would clear him of the charge. He was refused a hearing. Major X, who was in a position to secure a hearing for the priest, was appealed to, but refused to intervene.

The Cardinal told me that he had gone to great trouble and expense to get at the truth of the matter, and he had satisfied himself that the priest had been wronged. "If Major X comes here," said His Eminence, "I will tell him what I think of him. And apart from all this, you can tell Mr. de Valera not to worry over any activities of this man. If the leaders of the Church here are to be swayed, it will not be by Major X and, in any case, there are none of us who would like to see Ireland harmed."

After a few more interviews I found that Major X was making no headway whatsoever. Shortly afterwards, he abandoned his crusade.

About the same time I got a tip that an indictment against Ireland was being drawn up which would justify Allied intervention because of the widespread Nazi espionage in the country and the complacence of the Irish government regarding this supposed activity. The authors of the indictment, I was told, were Archibald McLeish, the poet, and Colonel William ("Wild Bill") Donovan of the famous 69th regiment. I sought out Mr. McLeish, with whom I had long been on friendly terms. He was at the time in charge of the Library of Congress. He was frankly astonished when he heard what I had to say. He said to me in effect:

"You should know better than to believe I would do anything to hurt Ireland. I have such esteem for Ireland and the Irish people that I would be the first to defend her. Anything I have been able to do in literature I owe entirely to the Irish poets, especially Yeats."

"And what about Colonel Donovan?" I asked.

"I don't know," he said, "he may be doing something of the sort, but I know nothing about it. I am not working with him on any project, but he did ask for some twenty or twenty-five members of my staff for his outfit, and he got them."

So I set out to see Bill Donovan, but that wasn't easy. For all of three weeks I was put off with excuses. He was sick, or he was away, or he was in conference. One day, having made sure that he was in the city and on the job, I went to his office. The receptionist told me that the Colonel was in conference. I said that I would wait there till the conference was over and that if I did not succeed in seeing him that day I would come back on the next day and the next day and that I would squat in the office until I saw him. This worked. In less than ten minutes I was brought into the office of the Director of the O.S.S. (The Office of Strategic Services), and I plunged into the subject straight away.

"I have been told," I said, "that you are drawing up a report on Nazi secret service activities in Ireland and that the contents of the report would justify an Allied invasion."

"That is not so," he said.

"You mean that there is no such report?"

"Well, no," he said, rather doubtfully.

"But you have stated," I said, "that there are many Nazi agents secretly working in Ireland."

"Yes," he said. "I have said that. It is fairly obvious, isn't it?"

"How is it obvious?"

"Well, look at the men who have been dropped by parachute."

"I have a list of them here," I said, taking the list from my pocket. "They have all been taken and their landing has been well publicised."

"What about those you have not taken?" he asked.

"You mean," I said, "that other German agents have been dropped by parachute and they have not been taken?"

"I don't know," he said, "whether they were dropped by parachute or not. I do know that there are a great many Nazi secret agents now at work in Ireland."

"Could you give me a list of them?"

"Why should I?"

"So that we could deal with them."

"No," he said. "That's a job for your government. They could find them if they wanted to."

"You think we don't want to find them?"

The Colonel merely shrugged at this.

"Look," I said, "we are desperately anxious to preserve our neutrality. In our own interest we must take all measures to defend it. We have given our word that we would not allow Ireland to be used against Allied interests. If you have any information regarding the activities of these supposed Nazi secret agents, don't you think you should give it to me?"

"Certainly not," he said. "You are a non-belligerent."

"All right," I said. "According to you the activities of these supposed Nazi agents are causing the loss of American and British lives."

"That is certainly so."

"Have you given the British—who are certainly not non-belligerents—the information I am asking for?"

"I have not."

"Then," I said, "you are neglecting your duty. If you gave the British this information, they would give it to us, and we could overnight sweep up all those Nazi spies and thus save the lives of thousands of British and American soldiers."

I knew I had cornered the Colonel. He hemmed and hawed and finally said:

"Listen. Let you and me get together on this. You come to lunch with me some day next week and we will go into the whole thing."

"Sure," I said. "That's all right with me."

Of course I knew that the call for the luncheon would never come. It never did. Wild Bill no more believed his own propaganda that did the sources from which it all emanated in Dublin. Their grievance was not that Ireland was overrun with spies, Nazi or otherwise. Their grievance was that Ireland was not in the war.

But as a result of my visit to Colonel Donovan, we never heard of any further adverse propaganda from that quarter.

In his memoirs, Cordell Hull writes:

In 1943 we faced two major questions in the development of our relations with Éire. One concerned the possibility of obtaining Irish bases, the other the possibility of inducing the Irish Government to demand the recall of Axis diplomats who, we had good reason to suspect, were passing on to their governments vital information they were able to obtain by virtue of being stationed so close to the shipping lanes and to Britain. On June 3rd, 1943, I wrote the President a memorandum enclosing suggestion along this line from Minister Gray in Dublin, who thought that a refusal of these requests should be met by a progressive shutting off by Britain and the United States of raw materials for Irish industries. The President wrote me on June 15:

> I have read David Gray's outline of views on American policy toward Ireland. What do you think we should do in regard to action? In the matter of asking for the use of ports, I think we might consider asking for a lease of the ports in a manner similar to the lease of the eight bases from Great Britain in 1940. However, the period could well be cut from ninety-nine years to the duration of the war. I think Mr. Gray is right in

> his desire to put De Valera on record. We shall undoubtedly be turned down. I think the strongest fact is that we are losing many American and British lives and many ships in carrying various supplies to Ireland without receiving anything in return, and without so much as a "Thank you". (p. 1355)

Here let me interrupt Mr. Hull. Of course in June 1943 I had no means of knowing the contents of the foregoing. At a later stage when it was openly stated that the Axis diplomats in Ireland were passing information to their governments, I held a press conference in the course of which I proved that there were no possible means by which the Axis diplomats could transmit any messages to their governments. Any letters they wrote could be scrutinised; any cables they sent had to pass through London; the only wireless set in the German Legation had been out of order from shortly after the war started. Later it had been taken away altogether by the Dublin government. Owing to the security measures taken by our government, the officials of the Axis powers might as well have been in the Sahara desert or at the North Pole so far as aiding the enemies of the Allied powers was concerned.

I was asked at this press conference if there could not be secret wireless sets in Ireland operated by the Germans. My reply was that any messages transmitted by such secret sets would have been at once intercepted by the Irish and British authorities, and the location of such wireless sets could have been found in a matter of hours.

The plan to blockade Ireland had been whispered about from time to time, but it was not taken very seriously by the Irish people, though the Government thought it not beyond the bounds of possibility. Mr. Hull, however, reveals that the project was seriously recommended by an official of the American government, who considered that the denial of Irish bases to the Allies and the refusal to banish the Axis diplomats "should be met by a progressive shutting off by Britain and the United States of raw materials for Irish industries". In other words, the Irish were to be starved out if they did not meet the allied demands.

Personally I cannot imagine a policy more futile. Any student of Irish history should have known that a threat to starve the Irish out would have produced a result far different from that intended.

Mr. Hull goes on:

I replied to the President that it appeared to me that without question air and naval facilities in Ireland would be of considerable usefulness to the United Nations' war effort. I added that a high officer of the War Department had informally advised us that these facilities would be enormously useful from a military standpoint. Prime Minister de Valera, however, I pointed out, had repeatedly declared that "there can be no question of leasing these ports" or "of handing them over on any condition whatsoever," and that any attempt by any of the belligerents to bring pressure to bear on the Irish Government to turn them over "could only lead to bloodshed." In making these statements, I said, Mr. De Valera no doubt had had principally in mind possible approaches from the British Government. Since our entry into the war, however, suggestions had been made that Ireland might be disposed to lease naval and air facilities to the United States.

"The Irish and the British", I said to the President, "have fought one another for seven hundred years. They suspect and distrust one another. Each tries on suitable occasions to obtain the support of the American people and Government against the other. We must be careful, therefore, to be sure that any action which we take in this regard has a sound military basis in the opinion of our own Chiefs of Staff. It seems to me that this is of fundamental importance to make it impossible for anyone to maintain that we took sides with the British against the Irish and "pulled British chestnuts out the fire."

I suggested that, since Ireland was at the back door of the United Kingdom and happenings inside Ireland were therefore of more immediate and direct interest to the United Kingdom than to the United States, we should first obtain the approval of the British Government.

I attached a draft letter for the President's signature, requesting the views of the Joint Chiefs of Staff on the military aspects of the question. Representatives of the War and Navy Departments designated by the Joint Chiefs of Staff advised us that they did not consider it possible at that time to foresee whether, with the progress of the war, we would actually desire bases in Ireland or exactly what military value such bases might have; but they did think it would prove of real help now in our strategic planning if we could be sure we would have the use of them if they were needed.

President Roosevelt and Prime Minister Churchill discussed the question of an approach to Ireland with regard to the bases at the time of the first Quebec Conference and later in the year at the Cairo Conference. Meantime I was in contact with Foreign Secretary Eden on the subject.

Finally on December 22, 1943, Eden gave us his Government's reply. He thought that Mr. De Valera would avoid a direct negative reply to any approach on the question of air and naval bases and would seek to cloud the issue by reiterating his grievances in regard to partition. Eden therefore believed that our proposed approach would be likely to give rise to acute difficulties and that it would be wiser to postpone it.

In a memorandum to the President on December 29 I said that, in view of this attitude by the British Government, I would let the matter rest unless he wished to discuss it further with Prime Minister Churchill."

In other words, it was the British and not the Americans who prevented the Allies from taking stringent measures against Ireland in 1943. No doubt this was because the British had had experience in Ireland and the Americans had not.

This leads me to another phase of American activities during the war, of which I knew nothing till the crisis had passed. An American officer who had served in the North of Ireland told me that shortly after the Americans landed in Derry, a zealous American officer attached to the U.S.H.Q. staff had drawn up a plan for the invasion and occupation of the twenty-six counties. According to this plan, the U.S. forces would take Dublin in less than two weeks and occupy the whole country in a few weeks more. The plan was sent to Washington, where it was considered by the State Department and by the army and navy chiefs. Finally, it got to London, where it was turned down by Anthony Eden. My informant said that the opinion in London was that the plan was on sound military lines, but what was the objective? If it was to secure the use of the Irish ports, it would not succeed. Though they might occupy the country and take the ports, they could not operate them because the Irish by tearing down the telegraph lines and tearing up the railways would make the position of the occupying forces difficult, if not impossible.

Mr. Hull says:

> In December, 1943, I received from Irish Minister Brennan two notes asking my support for Irish efforts to purchase two ships to replace those obtained from this country in 1941 and subsequently sunk. After consulting with Minister Gray in Dublin, I sent the President a memorandum on December 7th in which I suggested that we should refuse the Irish request on the grounds that our Government had previously chartered two merchant ships to Ireland, and that the Irish Government had permitted them to be sunk by Nazi submarines without offering the slightest word of protest to the German Government. Mr. Roosevelt approved (p. 1357).

This refusal was published and I was questioned by reporters about the matter. My reply received favourable publicity in the Irish papers. I said it was true that the two ships had been lost, but that neither Mr. Hull nor I had any knowledge that they had been sunk by Nazi submarines. One of them had simply disappeared and no one knew whether it had been sunk by a mine or by a submarine or by some other agency. The other had been probably sunk by a submarine which had been sighted by the crew the day before, but there was no means of knowing whether it was a German submarine or not. How in the circumstances could we protest to the German government? I instanced the case of the S.S. *Kerlogue*, an Irish ship, which had been machine-gunned from the air. The Americans, I pointed out, had loudly stated that the ship had been attacked by German planes flying from Brest, but an enquiry showed clearly that the attacking planes had been British. What sort of fools, I asked, would we have looked if before the enquiry we had protested to the Germans?

Towards the end of 1943 or the beginning of 1944, when the Allied forces were closing in on Rome, I was instructed to approach the U.S. government with the view of saving Rome from being bombed. I was to tell the State Department that my government would try to persuade the Germans to vacate the Eternal City so as to prevent its destruction by bombardment. I failed to get an appointment with the Secretary of State, but I did see Mr. Jimmie Dunn, one of the Assistant Secretaries. He was rather caustic. Did the Irish government not know that the U.S. government realised without being told what was involved in the bombing of Rome? The U.S. forces were fighting in the war and they did not have to be told by a neutral how they were to conduct it. They were as anxious as anyone to save Rome from being bombed, but if the Germans continued to use the city for military purposes, as they had been doing, there would be no way of saving the city from being bombed. I reported on this interview and stressed the resentful attitude of the State Department towards my representations. I was told, however, to pursue the matter further. I was aware that Archbishop Cicognani, the Apostolic Delegate to the U.S. from the Vatican, as well as the Spanish Ambassador, Francisco de Cardenas, had been making representations along the same lines, and I compared notes with them.

The next time I saw Mr. Dunn, he was somewhat more cooperative though still far from cordial. I realised that the representations made by my friends in Congress, whom I had kept posted on the question, were having some effect. Mr. Dunn said that the Apostolic Delegate had stated that the Italian forces had left Rome and that the German forces were about to do so. He added: "We are not so credulous as he is."

Mr. Hull says: "After receiving an appeal from Irish Prime Minister de Valera on April 3 (1944) the President replied on April 19th that if the German forces were not entrenched in Rome, no question would arise concerning the City's preservation" (p. 1563).

When I presented Dev's letter, Mr. Dunn went so far as to thank the Irish government for its interest in the matter and said that it now appeared that the city would be saved from bombing. When the Allies entered the city on 4 June, only the railway yards on the outskirts had been bombed, quite needlessly as it afterwards appeared.

In the spring of 1944 the most critical period of the war was at hand. The vast American forces in Britain and Northern

Ireland were being mounted for the invasion of the continent. Already it had been charged that the escape of two German battleships, the *Gniesau* and the *Breslau*, through the English Channel had been aided by weather reports received from Ireland. It was to be expected that any failure of the Allied expedition would be attributed to the fact that the Allies had not had control of all Irish territory. This was in the minds of the American administration when they demanded the expulsion of Axis diplomats from Ireland. Mr. Hull deals with the matter as follows:

In 1944 we took up actively with the Irish Government the question of the Axis diplomatic missions in Éire. On February 21, after co-ordinating our action with Britain, we made a formal request for their removal. We pointed out that Éire's neutrality was operating in favour of the Axis. One reason for this was the opportunity afforded to the Axis for highly organised espionage because of Ireland's geographical position.

Situated as you are, we said, in close proximity to Britain, divided only by an intangible boundary from Northern Ireland, where are situated important American bases, with continuous traffic to and from both countries, Axis agents enjoy almost unrestricted opportunity for bringing military information of vital importance from Great Britain and Northern Ireland into Ireland and from there transmitting it by various routes and methods to Germany. No opportunity corresponding to this is open to the United Nations, for the Axis has no military positions which may be observed from Ireland.

All this was of particular importance to us at that time because the United Nations preparations for the invasion of Normandy from Britain were approaching the climax, and we were making every effort to keep them secret.

Nevertheless, Prime Minister de Valera, in a note transmitted to us on 7 March, refused our request. He reasserted Éire's right to remain neutral, and he sought to prove that we had been misinformed in believing that Axis diplomats and agents were able to obtain and send from Ireland vital information concerning United Nations military activities.

One week later I cabled Ambassador Winant in London that we were considering a further message to Mr. de Valera. This would reaffirm the position we had taken in our original message and state that the American Government and people would inevitably hold the Irish Government responsible for actions against our forces and military operations taken by the Axis representatives in Éire. We felt, I said, that, without disclosing to the Irish Government whether we contemplated any further action, we should try to keep the question open. While we did not consider the use of economic sanctions advisable, I said I did not think we should commit ourselves, at least for the time being, not to use them, as both Minister Gray and the British representative in Dublin had suggested. However, I added, since Ireland obtained most of her supplies from Britain, this question was primarily a British one, and I requested Winant to obtain the views of the British Government.

The White House sent me on March 20 Britain's reply in the form of a message from Prime Minister Churchill to the President. Mr. Churchill, referring to my cable to Winant on the 14th, said that in his opinion it would be much better to keep the Irish "guessing for a while" than to offer them any immediate reassurances. He said he thought we should "let fear work its healthy process," and thereby we would get behind the scenes a continued stiffening up of Irish measures, which even then were not so bad, to prevent leakages of information.

Mr. Churchill said that, while Britain did not intend to stop necessary trade between England and Ireland, she did intend to prevent ships and airplanes from leaving Ireland for Spain, Portugal, and other foreign ports, and to restrict all communications to the utmost until the invasion of France had been launched. This was purely from the viewpoint of protecting American and British soldiers' lives and our military plans.

I sent the President on March 31 the reply which he had requested me to prepare. This stated his belief that Mr. Churchill was pursuing the right line in taking the security measures without, however, adopting measures of coercion designed only to harm Ireland. We wondered, however, if measures forbidding Irish ships to go to all foreign ports from Ireland might not be interpreted as economic sanctions and suggested they be permitted to continue to come to North America to carry wheat and other essential supplies to Ireland.

Mr. Churchill agreed.

We now planned to send a further note to Prime Minister de Valera concerning Axis representatives in Éire, and the President approved the text. The Irish Government, however, offered through our intelligence services to adopt whatever security safeguards we and the British desired in Ireland and Mr. Churchill told us he thought our first note had done great good and had prompted Irish authorities to strengthen their security measures but that a second note was not necessary. I sent the President a memorandum on May 17 proposing that we let the matter rest, to which he agreed (pp. 1357–8).

Regarding the foregoing, I had already made it clear that there was no "highly organised espionage" in Ireland on the part of the Axis powers, and that even if there was there were no means by which their information could be transmitted to Germany, Italy or Japan. The British knew this very well. They could have let the Americans know it also if they had wanted to do so. When Winston Churchill told F.D.R. that the Irish measures for the prevention of leakages "were not so bad", he was merely understating the case. With regard to Churchill's statement that Britain would prevent Irish ships and airplanes from leaving Ireland for Spain, Portugal and other foreign ports during the critical days before the invasion, anyone in Ireland would have readily agreed that this was a reasonable precaution. I certainly never heard a single complaint on that score. The salient point, however, in Mr. Hull's message to Winant, was that since the Irish had refused to accede to America's demands, "the American government and people would inevitably hold the Irish government responsible for actions against our forces and military operations taken by the Axis representatives in Éire." This, to my mind, can mean only that if for any cause the invasion failed, the Irish were to be blamed.

Mr. Hull says that before he had dispatched a further note to de Valera concerning Axis representatives in Ireland, "the Irish Government . . . offered through our intelligence services to adopt whatever security safeguards we and the British desired in Ireland. Mr. Churchill told us he thought our first note had done great good and had prompted Irish authorities to strengthen security measures."

This is really astonishing. The American government, if not the British, knew perfectly well in March 1944 that this self-same offer of the Irish government regarding security safeguards had been made about two years earlier and had been scoffed at.

Later the question of the ships we were still trying to buy came up again. I had continued to press for two general cargo ships to replace the *West Neris* (the *Irish Pine*) and the *West Hermatite* (the *Irish Oak*). Mr. Hull says:

> I sent the President a memorandum to give him my opinion on the question he had raised with us on May 9 (1944) as to whether two ships should be made available to the Irish Government. "We believe," I said, "That our request of the Irish Government that they expel the Axis representatives was a reasonable one with which they should have complied. We believe that public opinion in this country supported this request and in fact would be disposed to support pressure to cause Ireland to comply. The editorial reaction to this throughout the country was favourable. We believe that public opinion would find it difficult to understand our now making available two ships to get supplies to Ireland in view of the attitude which Ireland has taken toward us and the war (p. 1359).

It will be noted that the reason here given for the refusal of the U.S. government to let us buy two more ships was not that previously given. Then the refusal was based on the grounds that we had not protested to Germany about the sinking of the first two ships. Now the refusal was based on "the attitude which Ireland has taken towards us and the war".

Which, indeed, was the cause of all the trouble.

Mr. Hull states:

> During this period various Irish-American organisations urged the United States Government to use its influence with Great Britain to bring an end to partition between Éire and Northern Ireland, meaning that Northern Ireland would become a part of Éire. I adopted an attitude of complete impartiality on this issue, however, and Under-Secretary Stettinius stated our position on June 7, 1944, in a letter to Senator Danaher, as follows:
>
>> The Constitutional relationship between Northern Ireland and the Irish Free State is, of course, a matter for the proper authorities within the British Commonwealth to determine.

> The American Government could only take the position that the altering of political boundaries between the Irish Free State and Northern Ireland was not a matter in which it might properly intervene. International law and comity would permit no other course (p. 1360).

I am not an authority on international law. My wife and I used to attend every year in Washington a delightful banquet given by the International Law Society, and at one of them I asked an American luminary of the organisation what International Law consisted of. His reply was:

"Well, generally speaking, it's what you can get away with. In a sense it's like freedom of the seas, so much admired by the British and ourselves. In peace it means that you are free to sail the seven seas, provided you conform to the rules the British have laid down. In war it means you have no freedom at all unless you are on the British side—and since our interests are those of the British, we find it a convenient device."

As to "comity", the only definition I can find in *Websters Dictionary* is "mildness and suavity of manner; courtesy".

It would appear, therefore, according to Mr. Hull that neither international law, which, if my American friend was right, means expediency, nor comity, which means courtesy, could permit the U.S. government to intervene in the question of the partition of Ireland. Is it international law or comity which now compels the U.S. to insist on the ending of the partition of Germany? After all, the boundaries of Germany have changed very often in the past one thousand years, whereas the boundaries of Ireland were the same from time immemorial until forty years ago when the historic Irish nation was split in two by the act of a foreign power. Is it any wonder that the Irish are today cynical when they hear the mouthings of so-called statesmen?

When the war in Europe appeared to be coming to an end, the victors decided to go after the war criminals tooth and nail. They feared that the criminals (meaning of course the Germans and Italians and not at all the Russians) might seek asylum in a neutral country, as the Kaiser had done after World War One. The victorious Allies therefore decided to ask for guarantees from the neutral nations that they would not harbour the war criminals. All of the neutrals were warned that if any shelter or assistance or protection were given to the war criminals, it would be regarded as "a violation of the principles for which the United Nations were fighting and which they were determined to carry into effect by every means in their power."

In his book Mr. Hull sets out his dealings with the various neutral nations. They all sought to maintain the ancient right of asylum which had been held sacred for thousands of years, but, yielding to the threats of the big stick, all but one finally bowed down. Switzerland, Spain, Portugal, Sweden, Turkey and Argentina finally gave the necessary guarantees. The one exception was Ireland and maybe one day we will get credit for our stand.

Mr. Hull says:

> We had more difficulty with Éire, whom we approached on September 21 (1944). Prime Minister de Valera replied on October 9 that the Irish Government was unable to give assurances that would make it impossible for it to exercise its right to grant asylum should justice, charity, or the honor or interest of the nation so require. At the same time the Irish note declared that that Government did not intend to alter its practice of not admitting any aliens whose presence in Ireland would be contrary to Irish neutrality, detrimental to the Irish people's interests, or inconsistent with their desire to avoid harming the interests of friendly nations, and of deporting as soon as possible to their countries of origin any such aliens who might land.
>
> We did not consider this reply satisfactory. On October 23 we pointed out to the Irish government that we failed to understand how that Government could feel that charity, justice, or the interest or honor of Ireland could make necessary the admission of war criminals. We did not, however, obtain better assurances (p. 1363).

After October 1944, the pressure on Ireland eased off considerably. The rapid advance of the allied forces in Europe showing that ultimate victory in that area was only a matter of time, the transfer of interest to the Pacific war area, and the growing doubts in the minds of everybody, excepting, apparently, the Chief Executive and his advisers, as to the real aims of the Russians, pushed such questions as the attitude of the neutrals into the background.

There was an International Air Conference scheduled for Chicago in the autumn of 1944 to which we had accepted an invitation. There were some forty nations represented, including all the countries on the American continent, all the members of the British Commonwealth, most of the countries of Western Europe, and several countries in the Near and Middle East. The Russian government had accepted the invitation and their delegates had actually arrived in the U.S. when, for no reason given, they flew back to Russia instead of coming on to Chicago. The Yugoslav delegates who were present during the Conference actively defended the interests of the U.S.S.R.

The Irish delegation consisted of John Leyden, the Secretary of the Department of Industry and Commerce; Tim O'Driscoll and Dick Sullivan of the same Department; John Hearne, our Minister in Canada; Denis Devlin, Secretary of the Irish Legation; Garth Healy, our consul in Chicago; Thomas J. Monaghan, Chief Engineer of the Department of Posts and Telegraphs; and myself.

The proceedings had hardly got under way when, to their surprise, the delegates learned that the closest allies in the war were at daggers drawn. The U.S. and Britain were the main antagonists. Mr. Adolf Berle, the leader of the U.S. delegation, gave us an address in the course of which he said that it had taken centuries of bloody wars to achieve freedom of the seas. We could now achieve freedom of the air by ordaining that any country could fly anywhere and everywhere, picking up and setting down goods and passengers without any restrictions whatsoever.

Lord Swinton, the leader of the British delegation, was on his feet at once. He said quite bluntly that the policy advocated by Mr. Berle would be a grand one for the U.S.

"You have the planes," he said, "and the men to fly them. None of the rest of us have. If your policy is adopted, the U.S. will be enabled to collar all the air freight and air passenger services in the world and leave the rest of us high and dry."

Mr. Berle, in his reply, blandly ignored the arguments put forth by Lord Swinton. He said that if the conference missed its chance of establishing the principle of freedom of the air, it would be failing in its duty to mankind and the future.

The argument continued for several days. Then the principals decided to go into conference, which meant that the rest of us were left twiddling our thumbs while the British and the U.S. delegates debated behind closed doors. They debated for over two weeks and then they came out with a solution which was no solution at all because when Mr. Berle started to expound it in open session, Lord Swinton took exception to his interpretation and there we were back where we had started from.

The newspaper columnists got great fun out of my comment on the argument at this stage. I said it reminded me of a Laurel and Hardy picture where the two comedians having by prodigious efforts got a piano up a stairs, let it slide down to the bottom again.

The whole thing was at a complete deadlock when Mr. Sullivan, the delegate from New Zealand who was very popular with all the parties, asked me to intervene. He said that we were in the unique position of not having taken sides. He had sounded out the U.S. and British leaders, and they both would welcome my intervention. So we had the leaders of the U.S. and British delegations as well as Mr. Sullivan to lunch and the meal was an undoubted success, but not my efforts to bring about a more cordial and friendly atmosphere between the parties. As a matter of fact, a couple of days later, we heard that at a closed meeting there was a flare-up between the contending parties which left the atmosphere more bitter than ever. That night Lord Swinton took me aside and asked me how long I had known Mr. Berle. I said I had known him for several years.

"And what do you think of him?"

"I have always found him a courteous gentleman. I have never had any trouble with him."

"Well," said his Lordship, "what would you think of a man who one day makes a commitment and who utterly repudiates it the next day?"

"But surely," I said, "it's not the first time that a man's words have conveyed to his hearers a different interpretation than that which was in his mind."

"It's not a question of interpretation," said Lord Swinton. "The words were taken down by a stenographer and they could have had only one meaning. He denied that he had ever spoken the words."

That same night at a dinner I sat beside Mr. Berle. He told me that in order to meet Lord Swinton's case against a possible American monopoly of the air business he had offered to supply the British with all the machines and men they wanted for commercial air services, but that was not acceptable because Lord Swinton said that that would mean that Great Britain would be dependent on the U.S. for the maintenance, servicing and manning of the machines. He thought that that was an unreasonable attitude, but what riled him even more was that Lord Swinton had attributed to him statements he had never made.

"I never understood it before," said Mr. Berle. "But now I am beginning to see what you people must have been up against. I would hate to be small and weak and be confronted by that thing."

By "that thing" I gathered that he meant the British Empire.

"Well," I said, "we may be small, but we are not weak. And, after all, you must take into account the fact that Britain has been the predominant power in the world for several centuries, so they find it hard to have to take second place."

"They will have to face up to it," said Mr. Berle.

Next day Mr. Welch Pogue, the second in command in the American delegation, invited me to join him at lunch. He asked me if the Irish government would favour a bilateral agreement with the U.S. whereby they could fly to Shannon in exchange for the concession of the right of Irish planes to fly to U.S. airports. There was nothing in this proposal which was contrary to any procedure so far agreed upon at the conference. It had early been agreed that such regional agreements as the various countries wished to make could be fitted into such general agreements as might be arrived at. I told Mr. Welch Pogue that I would put the proposal to my government.

Our delegation considered the matter. We realised that Ireland was now very important for the Americans. The British had stated that unless there was agreement, they would deny them landing rights in Canada, Newfoundland or Bermuda, which meant, since at that time the limit for an uninterrupted flight was 2,000 miles, they could fly to Europe only if they could land in Ireland. The position was a ticklish one because if we agreed to the American request, and if afterwards the British and the U.S. should come to terms, we might find ourselves out in the cold. The instructions from Dublin, however, were to ask the Americans to put their proposal into writing. When they did so, Dublin agreed to go ahead on the basis of reciprocal landing rights. The agreement provided that all American planes bound to and from Europe should land at Shannon. It was to be completed by an exchange of letters in Washington.

The conference itself after five or six weeks of talk ended in all parties agreeing, as Mayor La Guardia stated, only to respect the red and green traffic lights.

Back in Washington, three or four weeks elapsed, but there was no sign of the completion of the agreement. Dublin was very anxious about the matter and so was I. At the State Department I was told that the matter was held up only because of the absence of the President from Washington. I saw Welch Pogue, who was head of the Aeronautics Board in the State Department. He was as angry as I was at the delay and plainly showed that he did not believe that the absence of the President was the cause of it. I told him that we had gone out on a limb in the endeavour to meet the wishes of the American administration and that now it appeared that they were going to let us down. He said he was still in hopes that he would get the thing through.

By this time Dublin was furious. They asked me if I thought publicity would help. Up to this time there had not been a whisper about the whole affair so far as the press and public were concerned, but we strongly suspected that a certain American official had given the whole thing away to the British. Indeed, we did not know at the time whether the delay was due to the opposition of the British or to the innate objections of some people in the administration who were still so sore at us because of our neutrality that they were willing to sacrifice U.S. interests rather than let Ireland have the credit of serving the interests of both.

I strongly advised against publicity. It could not possibly help, and it might well hinder. I told Welch Pogue of this and he agreed. He asked me to keep myself free for the weekend and to have my letter of acceptance of the agreement ready for signature. On the next day, Friday, he asked me to bring the letter to his office on the afternoon of the following day, Saturday. I did so. The letters were exchanged and the agreement completed. I understand that my cable announcing the news was made the occasion of a celebration in the Dublin office which, of course, I missed.

My wife and I were amongst the hundreds of diplomats, members of Congress and journalists who stood on the snow-covered ground behind the White House on 20 January, 1945 and listened to Roosevelt's inaugural address on accepting office for the fourth time. The President looked ghastly. He was plainly a dying man, and I found myself hoping that he would not collapse before he finished his speech. I was standing beside Mr. Bilmanis, the Minister for Latvia.

"How long do you give him?" I asked.

"Not more than six months," he said.

"My guess," I said, "is three months."

Actually he had less than three months to live. He died on 12 April, but meanwhile he had been to Yalta and back. The Russians apparently wanted to make sure he was dead because the Russian Ambassador, Mr. Gromyko, turned up at the State Department to say he had instructions to view the body. He was referred to the White House, where Mrs. Roosevelt showed him the door. Though everyone knew, in spite of the doctor's optimistic reports, that he had been a dying man, Franklin Roosevelt's death came as a shock to the American people. He had been for so long such a dynamic personality on the American scene that everyone felt there was a void. How could it be filled?

On the day he died, we were to go to an evening party given by a well-known Washington newspaperman. When my daughter Deirdre rang me to say that Roosevelt was dead, I naturally concluded that the party would be called off. I telephoned to my host and learned to my surprise that there was no intention of calling off the party. So off we went to find fifty or sixty people, members of Congress, army and navy officers, newspapermen, etc., in our host's house in Georgetown. The conversation was entirely about the new situation. What was the new guy like? The subject of the query, of course, was Harry Truman, who as Vice-President, would now become President.

My wife and I remarked afterwards that we did not hear one single person say a word of regret at the passing of F.D.R. That is not to say that there was no one there who regretted his departure. Indeed, there may have been many such. But it is typical of America that any concern with the past is a waste of time. F.D.R. was dead. He was now in the past. We can do nothing to alter or change the past. We may be able to do something about the future. What is the new guy like? Let us face the future.

EAMON DE VALERA

A MEMOIR

NOTE

It has long been an ambition of mine to write a life of Eamon de Valera, but I have never been able to get round to it and, moreover, I never got any encouragement from my intended subject. Once when we were travelling in a motor car in County Cork, I hinted at something of the kind, but his comment was discouraging. He suggested that biographers should wait till their subjects were dead, meaning that they might change their minds.

I have been of assistance to other writers who have dealt with this subject, and from time to time, I have jotted down some notes to be used in the work I had in mind.

Lately, when it was announced that An Taoiseach was to retire from the position he holds, I got out those notes and brought them up to date in the hope that the Editor of the *Irish Press* would publish them.

Now that I am in my eighty-first year, I have concluded that it was very unlikely that I should be able to carry out my original intention, so I decided to bring my notes up to date and let them go for what they are worth.

Robert Brennan

ONE

I well remember the first time I saw the name de Valera. It was in an issue of the *Irish Volunteer*, which, at the time, was printed in the office of the *Enniscorthy Echo*. The name appeared in a routine report of Volunteer activities in Dublin. I remember paraphrasing a few lines from Clarence Mangan:

> There's wine from the royal pope
> Upon the ocean green
> A Spanish gael shall give you hope,
> My Dark Rosaleen.

It was a couple of years later when I first saw Eamon de Valera. It was in Mountjoy prison where there were seventy or eighty prisoners marching around the exercise ring. The time was May 1916. We had all been tried by court-martial for our participation in the Rising, and many of us had received death sentences that had been commuted to various terms of penal servitude. Now we were awaiting our turn to be sent to serve our sentences in English convict prisons.

Apart from my Wexford comrades, who numbered half a dozen, I recognised none of the other prisoners in the parade, except Harry Boland, and I was glad when the latter dropped out of his place and fell in in front of me to get my account of what had happened in Wexford. Then he dropped out again and fell in behind me to give me his account of what had happened in Dublin. He himself had missed the mobilisation order but, on his way to Croke Parke for a hurling practice, he had heard the sounds of firing and he had made his way to the G.P.O., where he arrived with two members of the D.M.P. [Dublin Metropolitan Police], whom he had captured on the way. He was the same breezy, good-humoured Harry I had known for several years. You could not be gloomy or downcast in his presence. He indicated several of the other prisoners, identifying them. I was particularly struck by the appearance of a tall man with broad shoulders who walked with long strides and who looked unusually grave and dignified, in spite of the ridiculous prison clothes which were too small for him. Answering my question, Harry said that that was Eamon de Valera.

"The Spanish gael," I said.

"What's that?"

"It's an attempt at a joke," I said. "A Spanish Gael shall give you hope. My Dark Rosaleen."

"It's no joke," said Harry. "He put up the greatest fight of all of us in Dublin."

Harry gave me a brief account of the fight at Boland's Mill, where Dev was in charge of the Third Dublin Battalion and where, with fewer than a hundred men, he had held off a whole British army for the best part of a week. He said it was a miracle that de Valera had not been shot with the other leaders.

"Dublin was grand," said Harry. "No longer shall we hear Mitchell's jibe about the city of 'bellowing slaves and genteel dastards'."

It was about a week later when I saw de Valera again. This was in another prison yard, that of Dartmoor, in Devonshire. We walked around and around, four paces apart, and in his dignified, proud stride Dev seemed to exude contempt for his jailers. Any attempt to communicate with a fellow prisoner was rigorously punished. The warders swinging their batons watched relentlessly and, on occasion, armed guards appeared at the entrances to the yard, their guns at the ready.

At the time, we had not been provided with a workshop. There were about sixty of us and, during working hours, we sat on small individual stools three or four feet apart in the centre hall, making sandbags or mailbags. There was no chance of conversation under the vigilant eyes of the warders and there was a dead silence rule. The hall was gloomy, the warders forbidding, and after work when we were confined to our cells, one man to a cell, the silence was profound. One could take five short steps in the cell, no more.

After a few weeks of this treatment, though the majority of the prisoners remained buoyant enough, it was obvious from the strained look in their eyes that the regime was getting some of the prisoners down. All of these men had been active and uninhibited all their lives. They had just had experience of what was to them a cataclysmic upheaval in which they had risked their lives in a holy cause, they had gone through the noise and confusion of battle, they had seen their national flag raised on high only to be battered down by superior guns. But, even in defeat there was no despair. Indeed there was elation in the realisation that they had vindicated the national honour.

Then they were suddenly plunged into the icy silence and gloom of Dartmoor, denied communication with the outside world or even intercourse with their comrades. There were ten steel gates and ten sixteen-foot walls between them and the outside world and even that world in the immediate vicinity held nothing but the forbidding wastes of the moors of Devon. In all this there was the bitter thought that their leaders were as powerless as they were. They could do nothing for them. They, too, were chained in the iron discipline of the British penal system.

No wonder there was gloom and downheartedness amongst the prisoners.

One well-remembered morning, this atmosphere was changed with startling suddenness and it vanished, never to return. The change was due to an inspired action taken by Eamon de Valera, which revealed at once his chivalry, daring and defiance.

Eoin McNeill's trial by court-martial took place two or three weeks after we had arrived in Dartmoor. He received a life sentence. Denied all access to newspapers, we knew nothing of this until one morning, when we were lined up as usual in the main hall for counting. Despite the silence rule, the whisper went round that McNeill had arrived in the prison the night before. After we had been counted, we did not get the usual order to march off to the exercise ground and there was a long silence. I was obvious that something unusual was about to happen and there was an air of expectancy. Suddenly we heard a noise on the second landing and, looking up, saw McNeill with a warder about to descend the iron stairs.

Of course we all knew that there were mixed feelings about McNeill. By his action in countermanding the orders of the Military Committee he had prevented the Rising from being nationwide. I would not say there was active hostility towards him, but there was little cordial feeling. Yet, here he was now, a man far older than many of us, one who, a scholar amongst scholars, had given lifelong service to Ireland; here he was now, arrayed in the garb of a convict, caught in the toils of the ancient enemy.

De Valera stepped from the ranks and faced us. His voice rang out: "Irish Volunteers, attention!" The order was so promptly obeyed that it sounded like the click of a single pair of heels.

Again came Dev's voice: "Irish Volunteers, eyes left!"

Again the order was obeyed. Not a word was spoken but one could feel the sense of elation and pride that swept the vast hall almost like a flame.

As McNeill took the place in the ranks assigned to him by the warder, Dev gave the order: "As you were." Principal Officer Stone said to him, almost gently:

"All right, come along," and he and Dev walked out of the hall.

Amongst us there was no outward jubilation, but a quiet feeling of intense joy. We could still be what Yeats was later to call "the indomitable Irishry". Not the least amongst us but would have been willing to face the triangle to which we feared Dev was headed, for we all knew that the penalty for mutiny, such as this was, was the lash.

However, wiser counsels prevailed. The priest told the Governor that he was faced with an unprecedented situation wherein sixty men would, on an order, act as one man, with unknown consequences. It would certainly lead to the disruption of prison discipline and there was no knowing what the reaction of the two thousand ordinary convicts would be.

De Valera was back with us next morning.

TWO

If I dwell on those early prison scenes, it is because in those prisons there was brought into existence the inner core of the formidable and splendid Republican organisation which served Ireland so well from 1917 to 1921.

From the moment he gave the salute to McNeill, Dev was our unquestioned leader. Later there was an election, but it was only a matter of form. No one questioned his authority and, if there was any criticism, it came from those who were impatient for action and who thought that Dev was not moving fast enough. But he was patient and cautious and calm. He would strike only when he deemed the time ripe and a prerequisite was that the people at home were to be fully informed when the struggle was at hand. While we were in Dartmoor, there was little chance of setting up the Dublin liaison, which was so vital. Consequently, many weary, monotonous months elapsed without a break and then it came one day without any planning.

Dev was caught in the act of passing a six-ounce loaf to a hungry comrade. He was brought before the Governor and sentenced to three days in the solitary cells. He promptly went on hunger strike. In excited whispers we were debating whether we should strike in sympathy, when word came that Dev and two companions, Dr. Dick Hayes and Desmond Fitzgerald, had been whisked away to another prison. Thereafter all discipline went to pot and it was clear that only a short time would elapse before the whole system would break down. The British authorities played into our hands.

They decided to bring all the Irish political prisoners to Lewes jail, in Sussex.

Here there were one hundred and twenty-five of us and, after a few weeks, we held an election and Dev was chosen leader by an all but unanimous vote. He accepted the decision with his usual grave dignity. He knew that the office involved responsibility, with a possible terrible outcome. He realised that this band of Irishmen would not indefinitely meekly bear the criminal badge the British government had pinned on them. Though the vast majority of the prisoners accepted, without hesitation, his authority and respected his judgment, there were a few who were constantly urging him to take some decisive action to bring a well-nigh intolerable situation to an end. To those Dev would talk patiently, using all his powers of logic and commonsense and, invariably, he won them to his viewpoint. There was, however, in the prison a very small group who questioned, not so much his judgment, or his decisions, but his authority. He resented this attitude bitterly. He held that since authority had been freely bestowed on him by his comrades, every man was bound in duty and in honour to recognise it, otherwise there would be chaos and perhaps disaster.

There was never much real danger from this small group and I mention it only to show how faction can rear its ugly head, even in the most unlikely places.

In Lewes jail we jogged along for several months with only occasional flare-ups, arising mostly from contests of wits between some overly officious English warders and over-adventurous Irish prisoners. Always Dev preached patience and restraint. Most of us did not know that already he had a line of communication with the leaders in Dublin whom he kept fully informed of the situation in the jail. Few of us knew that he was eagerly awaiting the precise moment when an outbreak on the part of the prisoners would have such a repercussion in Ireland that our demand for treatment as prisoners of war could not be denied.

Once more the British authorities played into our hands. On arriving at Lewes jail we had been informed that we should enjoy a special privilege, that of talking during exercise. Of course we had taken advantage of this concession by talking before and after exercise and, indeed, at all times. Discipline became so slack that the Home Office decided to take action. They sent down an official who had us all assembled in the central hall, where he harangued us. He reminded us that the permission to talk had been a concession and not a right. It had been abused, and such behaviour could no longer be tolerated. In future, we could talk at exercise but during the rest of the time we would have to obey the prison rules on silence. Otherwise, this concession would be withdrawn, as would some others, such as extra letters, etc.

When he had finished reading a long document, Dev spoke up.

"On behalf of the prisoners," he said.

The official raised his hand:

"Silence," he said. "No one is allowed to speak on behalf of the prisoners. March them off to their cells."

So off to the cells we were marched.

That night Seumas Brennan, one of our comrades who served Mass and looked after the altar, brought me a message in Dev's perfectly neat handwriting. He said that when we were paraded for exercise next morning he would present to the Governor a formal demand for our rights. Next morning, when we were lined up there was an air of suppressed excitement. There was an unusually large number of warders on duty. The Governor, a prematurely aged, sad man, stood a little distance off and Stone, the principal warder, was white as chalk. After we had been counted, the order to march off was given, but we all stood still.

Dev stepped from the ranks, approached the Governor, and handed him a paper, saying:

"We, the Irish Republican prisoners, demand to be treated henceforth as prisoners of war or political prisoners. If our demand is not granted forthwith, we shall refuse to accept the status of convicts, we shall refuse to obey the prison rules, we shall not work, and we shall not associate with the convicts."

When Dev had finished, the Governor nodded to Stone, who gave the order to march back to our cells. There was much speculation amongst us as to what was to be the next step. We had not long to wait and those who had been nagging Dev because he did not take decisive action certainly had nothing to complain of in the next few days. Dev sent me a note to say we were to make a demonstration by destroying everything breakable in our cells, starting with the windows. I was to give the signal for our wing at eight o'clock that night by singing "God Save Ireland" from my window.

Punctually at eight I started the song. It was chorused by all the prisoners in the wing and when it ended the smashing of the windows began to the accompaniment of wild cheering. The people of the usually peaceful town of Lewes, attracted by the noise, assembled outside the prison walls. We were told that a whole horde of press correspondents from London flocked to the scene, but under the dictates of the Defence of the Realm Act, their reports were suppressed. The news got out in Dublin, however, and all over the country there were meetings and demonstrations on behalf of the prisoners, despite edicts and proclamations and baton charges.

On the next night we had a similar demonstration, smashing the glass panes of the light, the spy-holes in the door and so on. Next we started taking down the walls between the cells and, it is safe to say, that within a week the prison would have been a complete wreck had not the authorities decided to call a halt. In small groups and in chains, we were taken from Lewes and brought to various prisons all over England, where we continued the fight.

We did not know it at the time, but the fight was already won. The introduction of these rebels into the various prisons threatened to have a disastrous effect on the whole British penal system. In Parkhurst, on the Isle of Wight, for instance, where I was located, the Governor was advised that the example of the Irish rebels—we had mutinously marched off the exercise ground in the presence of fifteen hundred convicts—was having a profound effect on the convicts and an outbreak might be expected at any moment.

So, on the fifteenth of June [1917], Mr. Bonar Law announced in the House of Commons that the Irish prisoners were to be released right away, and so we were. With unerring judgment de Valera had chosen the right moment to strike.

THREE

As we walked, free men once more, out of the portals of Pentonville Prison in London, Dev was handed a telegram. It was an invitation to him to contest the East Clare vacancy caused by the death in France of Major Willie Redmond. This was a challenge. He had been looking forward to a return to the calm academic atmosphere of Blackrock and to a quiet life in the bosom of his family. He had no longing for the hustings. In fact, he had never stood on a political platform. A plunge into the sea of Irish politics, often murky, and, indeed, sometimes turbulent, if not tempestuous, held no lure for him. On the other hand, was not this a clarion call to duty? Clare, the Banner county, had a proud tradition. It was the gallant sons of the Dalcassians who, in the face of impossible odds, had ninety years earlier elected Dan O'Connell to the British parliament and opened the gates to emancipation. Would not Clare show the way again and lead to victory on a bigger field?

The immense crowds assembled at Westland Row to welcome the prisoners back to Ireland had waited all night long. The scenes of enthusiasm were beyond anything any of us had ever seen. It seemed as if all Dublin, and, indeed, all Ireland was there. The Volunteers were quite unable to gain for the prisoners a free passage. I was close to Dev as we emerged from the station. He must have been as much moved as the rest of us, but he showed no signs of emotion. He set his jaw and said to no one in particular:

"Look, we must win that election."

In those words was the implication that he, at least, would not let those grand people down. He had made his choice. For good or ill, he was to become the standard bearer of a resurgent Ireland.

After the election he said to me that before he stepped on the platform he had had many talks with the people of Clare.

"The young men urged me to be cautious and to use restraint. The old men, however, said, 'Make no mistake. Nail the flag of the Republic to the mast and never let them haul it down.' I took the advice of the old men."

The people of Clare, hearing him for the first time, were puzzled. They had been used to fiery speeches from the political platform. For a generation the flamboyant oratory of the brothers Redmond, John and Willie, had held them spellbound. If they expected anything of the kind from this tall, young, scholarly looking candidate, they must have got a shock. There was no sunburstry, no great round of periods of eloquence. Indeed, the young man who faced them spoke awkwardly, without emotion, and almost without emphasis. But they listened and sensed his earnestness and sincerity, the iron steadfastness behind his words, the resolute determination to carry the national struggle to victory.

Lloyd George was to say at the end of the campaign:

"I have read his speeches. They are not excited and so far as the language is concerned, they are not violent. They are plain, deliberate, and, I might almost say, cold-blooded incitements to rebellion."

It was the language the people wanted to hear. Before he had been speaking ten minutes, the audience realised that they were listening to a leader and that Clare and all Ireland had found a champion worthy of the race. The people of Clare gave this young man, hitherto unknown to them, five thousand votes and only two thousand for his opponent, a well-liked local man whom they had known all their lives.

About this time Alice Milligan wrote a little poem addressed to Dev. I remember only a few lines of it:

Back from the jaws of death
As came Tirconnell's Hugh
And the legions of the Gael have risen
To follow after you.

After the election, de Valera was co-opted a member of the National Executive of Sinn Féin, the open political organisation into which a huge number of Republicans had flocked after the Rising. Not all those who joined were enthusiastic about either the name Sinn Féin or its objectives, particularly its immediate objective, which was to secure the restoration of the Constitution of 1782, embracing as it did "the King, Lords, and Commons" of Ireland, but it was the only open political organisation which was close to their line of advance and they were determined to alter its constitution. At any rate, it denied the right of Britain to rule Ireland and it was fiercely opposed to the policy of sending the elected representatives of Ireland to the British House of Commons.

Within the newly augmented organisation there were wide and seemingly irreconcilable differences, which threatened to split it. De Valera took on himself the task of reconciling those differences. He wanted to build a broad national movement in which all the forward forces of the nation, the I.R.B., the Irish Volunteers, Sinn Féin, the Liberty League, the National Volunteers, Cumann na mBan, etc., would be formed into a phalanx whose combined force would be irresistible. Many doubted that he could succeed, even though he already had, by sheer patient logic, convinced the Volunteers that in the interests of national unity Eoin McNeill and his many followers throughout the country should be restored to their full confidence.

The annual Sinn Féin Ard Fheis was almost upon us and still agreement seemed to be a long way off. Cathal Brugha was determined that he would not work with Griffith or with any man who did not clearly state from the outset that his objective was an Irish republic. Griffith was equally adamant in standing by the original constitution of Sinn Féin, the organisation he had brought into existence. We seemed to be heading for a bitter fight and a split. At one meeting of the Executive, Brugha defied Griffith and said that if the latter embarked on a nationwide campaign, he would see that the Volunteers would prevent him from holding a single meeting in any part of Ireland.

It is now [*c.* 1958, when this memoir was written] over forty-one years since those momentous days and I can say now, as I said then, that but for de Valera the cause would have been lost, there and then, in a disastrous split. Dev had been working night and day trying to arrive at an agreed solution. Patiently he brought to bear on the protagonists of the opposing camps that clear and shining logic which is one of his outstanding gifts and, finally, he got them to agree on a definition of the aims of the new Sinn Féin organisation. It should aim to secure the recognition of Ireland as an independent Irish Republic and when we had achieved that status, the Irish people could by referendum freely choose the form of government they wished.

This clause was embodied in the new Constitution, which was submitted to the Ard Fheis and passed unanimously. During the meeting, however, Dev, who was speaking in support of the resolution, suddenly said, apparently as an aside:

"And if we choose an alternative form of government than that of a republic, and if we, for instance, choose a king, we are very sure that he will not come from the House of Windsor."

It was the high point in a day of vast excitement. The delegates rose and cheered for many minutes and thereafter everything seemed almost an anticlimax, even when Arthur Griffith and Count Plunkett, who had both been nominated for President, each withdrew his candidacy in favour of Dev. Griffith in proposing de Valera said: "He is a man in whom you will have a statesman as well as a soldier."

Two days later Dev was unanimously elected President of the National Executive of the Volunteers. He was thus in the pre-eminent position of having charge of both the military and civil branches of the movement. It was a unique position embracing great strength, but carrying tremendous responsibility.

There were those who asked if this young man, without training or experience, could measure up to it. For those of us who already knew him, there was not a shadow of a doubt.

FOUR

In 1918 few people in Ireland would have denied the fact that de Valera played a major part in defeating the plans of the British government to apply the Conscription Act to Ireland. There were, however, few who knew that it was his contribution which was the vital factor in deciding the issue in favour of Ireland, as a result of which, for the first time in 136 years, the will of the Irish people prevailed over that of the British government.

It is doubtful if there was ever such a unity of feeling and purpose amongst the Irish people as that which existed in the spring of 1918. It is true, of course, that the Unionist leaders were not represented at the Mansion House Conference, but it is equally true that the followers of the Unionists were as much overjoyed at the outcome of the Conference as were the rest of the people, north, south, east, and west.

The British had long been threatening to extend the Conscription Act to Ireland. People here had come to believe that their hesitancy was due to fear of the immediate consequences in Ireland and of the subsequent repercussions outside Ireland and especially in America. There were diehards in the hard core of British Unionism, led by Sir Henry Wilson, who kept sniping at Lloyd George for his failure to avail of the resources of manpower which Ireland held and which might relieve the terrific pressure of German forces on the Western Front. Sir Henry, who was Chief of the Imperial Staff, said he was "not afraid to take 100,000 to 150,000 recalcitrant, conscripted Irishmen into an army of over two million fighting in five theatres of war."

The discussions over the issue had been loud and long, but in March 1918, they had died down to such an extent that the people began to hope and believe that the crisis had passed. Not so, however. On 9 April 1918, the British government introduced a measure for the immediate application of the Military Service Act to Ireland.

Everyone wondered why this decision should have been reached at that particular time. Only a week earlier, President Wilson had solemnly warned Lloyd George that such a step might cause trouble in the United States. It was rumoured that the British authorities had been led to believe that the Irish bishops, while making it clear that they were against the Act, would discountenance any but passive resistance. Dev held that any such line would merely invite disaster. If the British thought that they would meet only passive resistance, they would go ahead with their plans and Ireland would be plunged into bloodshed, because the young men would resist by force in any event.

The effect in Ireland of the British decision was immediate. All closed ranks. The Irish Party in the House of Commons protested passionately, but in vain. The proposal was carried by a vote of three to one, whereupon John Dillon took the step which Arthur Griffith had been urging him to take for years. He led the Party out of the House of Commons and they returned to Ireland to organise resistance.

At the Mansion House Conference convened by Lord Mayor Larry O'Neill to meet the menace, the Irish Party was represented by John Dillon and Joe Devlin; the All for Ireland League by William O'Brien of Cork; the Independent Parliamentarians by Tim Healy; Labour by William O'Brien of Dublin, Michael Egan, and Tom Johnson; and Sinn Féin by Griffith and de Valera.

To those of us who knew him it was no surprise to learn that Dev dominated the proceedings right from the start. William O'Brien, M.P., stated so while paying a tribute to Dev's "transparent sincerity", his "gentleness and equability", and "the obstinacy with which he would defend a thesis." It was Dev who drew up the pledge to be taken by the people:

"Denying the right of the British government to enforce compulsory service in this country, we pledge ourselves solemnly to one another to resist Conscription by the most effective means at our disposal."

This pledge was taken by practically every citizen over eighteen in every parish in Ireland on the following Sunday. In many cases, all the people of the parish, headed by a band and young men and women carrying the Tricolour, marched en masse to the parish church to sign the pledge. The scenes of enthusiasm were tremendous. Old men and women who had not left their mountain homes for years came down to cheer the young men and women on. Within a few days a specially called Trade Union Congress comprising fifteen hundred delegates decreed a twenty-four hours strike as a protest against Conscription. Outside of Belfast, the strike was a hundred per cent successful. Anyone who lived through the period will remember the sound of footsteps. No other sound was heard in the streets. All traffic was at a standstill. All factories and shops were silent. No newspapers appeared and in the hotels the guests had to wait on themselves. Labour had demonstrated its power and had shown what it could do if the Act were enforced.

From the Mansion House there also came the following declaration, drawn up by Dev and unanimously adopted:

Taking our stand on Ireland's separate and distinct nationhood and affirming the principle of liberty that the governments of nations derive their just powers from the consent of the governed, we deny the right of the British government or any external authority to impose compulsory military service in Ireland against the clearly expressed will of the Irish people. The passing of the Conscription Bill by the British House of Commons must be regarded as a declaration of war on the Irish nation.

The alternative to accepting it as such is to surrender our liberties and to acknowledge ourselves slaves.

It is in direct violation of the rights of small nationalities to self-determination which even the Prime Minister of England—now preparing to employ naked militarism and force his Act upon Ireland—himself officially announced as an essential condition for peace at the Peace Congress. To attempt to enforce it will be an unwarrantable aggression, which we call upon all Irishmen to resist by the most effective means at their disposal.

It will readily be seen that de Valera had his eye on America when he drew up this Declaration.

But it was in Maynooth that the most telling and decisive blow was struck against Conscription. If, as had been rumoured, Lloyd George had banked on the bishops' outlawing any except passive resistance, he must have got a rude shock. By a most extraordinary and fortunate coincidence (an old priest said to me at the time, "Can't you say it was by the Grace of God?") it happened that on the first day of the Mansion House Conference, the bishops were also holding their annual meeting at Maynooth and everyone expected a pronouncement from them on the crisis. The Conference sought and obtained an audience. A deputation consisting of the Lord Mayor, John Dillon, William O'Brien (the Labour man), Tim Healy and Dev hastened to Maynooth. There was a profound sigh of relief when the bishops' manifesto appeared almost immediately. Its terms were clear and unequivocal: "We consider that conscription forced in this way upon Ireland is an oppressive and inhuman law which the Irish people have a right to resist by every means that are consonant with the law of God."

The battle was won. The young men who really longed for a trial of strength against the ancient enemy in a cause which had the support of the whole Irish people were no longer to be shackled by the fear of moral condemnation or prescription. They were free to meet the foe in a clear atmosphere where the bishops and the Fenians could join hands in a holy cause.

The British government continued to make believe that Conscription still loomed over Ireland, but no one in Ireland was deceived. The issue was settled. As I have said in the beginning of this chapter, for the first time in 136 years the will of the Irish people prevailed over that of the British government.

FIVE

Somewhere in his *Life of Parnell* Barry O'Brien says (it is over fifty years since I first read the book, and I have been unable to find the passage during the past few days, so I am quoting from memory) "The most amazing thing about this amazing man (Parnell) was that whenever you put a proposition before him, however new, you found that he had had it in mind a long time before it had occurred to you and that he had already considered it and had made his decision."

Thomas Carlyle has much to say on this subject in, I think, *Heroes and Hero Worship*. His theory as well as I am able to recall it after fifty years or so was that a leader was one who could see farther than the rest of us, and that was why he became a leader.

That may be so.What is certain is that during the few weeks I worked closely with Dev in the spring of 1918, I found that he had the same extraordinary foresight that Barry O'Brien had attributed to Parnell. Not once but many times, I came in with a bright idea, quite new, only to find that he had thought of it a long time before and that was not only my experience. Many of his visitors older and far shrewder than I was found the same thing.

We were housed in an office on the third floor of 6 Harcourt Street and how I came to be there is a story which throws a light on another side of Dev's character. After the Rising and the general release of the prisoners in June 1917, I returned to Wexford, but early in the following year, after a sojourn in Cork jail, I attended a meeting of the Ard

Chomhairle of Sinn Féin in Dublin. Dev, who was in the chair, called me aside during the meeting and told me that the Executive was thinking of setting up a Sinn Féin Press Bureau. Did I know anyone who would be suitable to be put in charge of it? All they could offer was £3 a week. I suggested a couple of names, but he did not seem impressed. That night when I got back home to Wexford, Una listened to my account of the proceedings and when I came to the matter of the Press Bureau, Una surprised me by saying:

"Don't you think he meant you?"

"Surely not," I said. "He would have said so. He knows he has only to hold up his finger, and I would be with him."

"All the same," she said, "I think he meant you."

That night I wrote to Dev and said that if he meant me, I was willing to take the job right away, and in a week or so I was appointed. This decision reveals the characteristic I speak of. Dev has always been reluctant to place a burden on anyone. He undoubtedly knew that a wish from him was a command for me and, in fairness to me, he did not want to issue what would have been tantamount to an order. He wanted me for the post, but to obtain it I should freely volunteer.

In addition to writing a weekly Sinn Féin column of notes for the provincial papers (which was successful beyond my hopes), I was collecting material to annotate the case against Conscription which Dev at the instance of the Mansion House Conference was drawing up to be presented to President Wilson by the Lord Mayor. This document had not been completed at the time of the "German Plot" arrests, but even it its incomplete state I had it printed and published by Maunsel and Roberts.

As for the "German Plot", no one now doubts but that it was originally designed for a twofold purpose. It would make Conscription easier by removing the Irish leaders and help to poison American opinion against us by linking Ireland with the German enemy. No one in Ireland believed that there was a German plot. A Clareman named Joseph Dowling, who had been a member of Casement's Brigade, was put ashore on the Galway coast from a German submarine. It was later learned that the Germans had put him ashore for the purpose of trying to establish communication with Sinn Féin. Apart from this there was never any evidence of a German Plot, but on this flimsy evidence, Lloyd George arrested almost the entire executive of Sinn Féin and the leaders of the Volunteers throughout the country. Without trial, they were all interned in English prisons.

Mick Collins, who had already set up his very efficient intelligence service, said that the arrests would take place on the night of 17 May and, on that night, the Executive held a meeting at which it was decided that the members would not go on the run. Every member nominated a substitute who would act in his or her absence. That night Dev was arrested. From that time little was heard of him until 3 February 1919, when his sensational escape from Lincoln Jail made ribbon headlines in the English papers.

Of course no one would wish to minimise the part played by Mick Collins, Harry Boland, Frank Kelly and the others who participated in the escape, but that is no reason why the part played by Dev himself should be overlooked. The fact is that the brilliant escape plan was his and that it was he who did the necessary preliminary work without which it could not have succeeded. He was the man who served Mass in the prison chapel and, in the course of his duties, he had much to do with candles and occasionally was in the vicinity of the chaplain's prison keys. With the aid of some candle ends and much ingenuity, he managed to get a wax impression of the keys. He then got a fellow prisoner, Sean Milroy, to draw what purported to be a comic postcard that was mailed openly to a friend in Dublin. This postcard passed in Dublin from Billy to Jack until finally someone looking at it one day saw its serious purpose. It gave the exact measurements in two drawings of a key. Naturally, coming from such a source, it could only be a prison key. So a duplicate key was made in Kilkenny.

When the night set for the escape arrived, everything worked smoothly. The movements of those within the gates and those without had been splendidly planned to coordinate. But when those without inserted the key in the gate and turned it, it snapped off, the handle remaining in Collins's hand and the head of the key in the lock. It was a dreadful moment and the men outside, Collins, Boland and Kelly, began to swear. Dev, however, produced another key. He had thoughtfully provided himself with a spare. Carefully, oh so carefully, he introduced this into the lock and, to his intense relief, found that the broken head of the first key remained in the upright position. He pushed it and turned his own key and the lock shot back. He and his two companions, Sean Milroy and Sean McGarry, were free.

This unsuspected ingenuity of his recalls to my mind some previous examples. Here is one. During the fighting at Boland's Mill in 1916, there was a tall factory chimney which obstructed the line of fire of the Volunteers. Dev wanted to blow it up but he could not spare the explosives, so he decided to get the British to take it down for him. He climbed the chimney and affixed the Tricolour to the top of it. Thereafter the British shelled the chimney and though they hit it frequently they never succeeded in quite demolishing it. At the end of the week there was hardly a brick on brick, but the Tricolour still proudly waved at the top. Incidentally, the exploit almost cost Dev his life. When he had secured the flag to the top of the chimney, he suddenly remembered that he had to get down and that he had no head for heights. He knew that if he looked down he was finished. So he kept his eye on the flag up aloft while he cautiously felt his way down the all too steep ladder.

"When I reached the ground," he said, "it was as much as I could do to remain upright."

After his escape from Lincoln jail, nearly two months elapsed before Dev returned to Dublin. It was deemed safer that for the present he should lie low in England. Early in March the dreaded 'flu of that awful year (1919) struck and many of the prisoners were affected. One of them, Pierce McGann, the deputy for Mid Tipperary, died in Gloucester jail and forthwith all the Irish prisoners were released.

Dev came back to Dublin and on the day of his arrival Cathal Brugha decided he should be driven to his home in Greystones and I went with them. On the way I was given a glimpse of another trait of Dev's which then, and later, irritated his colleagues very much. It was his Spartan hatred of spending a penny of public money needlessly. We were driving up Harcourt Street when he told Brugha to halt the car at Harcourt Street Station.

"What's the matter?" asked Brugha.

"I can take the train here," he said.

"Ah, for God's sake," said Brugha. "Sit back there and relax."

The car went on but I could see that Dev was very much upset at the idea of needlessly spending public money on a car drive from Dublin to Greystones when there was a cheaper mode of travel available. He was not comforted even when I told him he would have had to wait an hour or more for a train.

SIX

In a letter from Mountjoy Jail written a few short weeks before he was to fall before a firing squad, Liam Mellowes wrote:

> The time has come for informing the Irish people what miracles de Valera accomplished there [in America]. The attempt to belittle his work for Éire both here and abroad must be defeated. Show how it was . . . that de Valera changed an ignorant and either apathetic or hostile people into genuine sympathisers in two years. He made the name of Ireland respected where it was despised and the Irish cause an ideal where it had been regarded as political humbug.

I deliberately chose those words of Mellowes to head this chapter because Dev's visit to America in 1919–1920 has been so beclouded by falsehoods and misrepresentations that even today, nearly forty years later, the real picture has remained blurred. Mellowes was a man who hated hypocrisy, falsehood, and untruth. He was on the spot when de Valera arrived in America and was with him all the time of his sojourn there. He, more than any other man, was in a position to judge the effect of the impact which Dev's arrival made on America and the results of his campaign in that country. The attempts to belittle those results and to misrepresent them cut Mellowes to the quick and that is why he wrote the letter quoted above.

At the time Mellowes wrote the letter, it had been stated that on his visit to America, Dev caused a split. The simple truth is that there was already a split there and it was wide and deep. So wide and deep, indeed, that Dev did not realise the task he had undertaken when he volunteered to go to

America to heal it. It was only one of his tasks but, in his mind, it was only a minor one. He was to find out that it was and remained a major one.

After the General Election of 1918, the setting up Dáil Éireann as the government of the Irish Republic, the escape of Dev from Lincoln Jail and his subsequent election as President of the Republic, it was clear to him and to his advisers that he would have to enlist the aid of a powerful friend in the world forum if he was to secure the international recognition of that Republic. It was already obvious that Britain would stop at nothing in her endeavour to crush the resurgent Irish nation. The raids and arrests in the dead of night of Sinn Féin leaders and sympathisers, and the suppression of every newspaper which published the Dáil advertisement for the internal loan, were but a foretaste of the British terror which was to come.

America had emerged from the war, potentially if not actually as the most powerful nation in the world. Her foremost spokesman had declared unequivocally that chief amongst the war aims should be the right of all nations, great and small, to self-determination. The Peace Conference which was to lead to the formation of the League of Nations was sitting in Versailles. Dáil Éireann had appointed three delegates, de Valera, Griffith and Count Plunkett, to attend the Conference.

An Irish Race Convention held in Philadelphia on 22 February 1919, which was attended by distinguished Prelates of the Catholic Church in the United States and Canada, by Protestant and Jewish leaders and by outstanding Federal and State officers throughout the U.S., passed a resolution calling on the Peace Conference to give a hearing to the Irish delegates and appointed three prominent Americans, Frank P. Walsh of Kansas, ex-Governor Dunne of Illinois and Michael J. Ryan of Philadelphia to go to Paris to urge President Wilson's support for Ireland's claim. They failed in this mission. In a pathetic scene in Paris, Wilson confessed that he was powerless to carry out his war promises about small nations. The big four, Britain, France, Italy and the U.S.A., had decided that no claims on behalf of any small nation could be heard except by the unanimous consent of the big four.

The American delegates came to Ireland and were accorded a terrific reception. Dev told them that what was wanted in America was a campaign to secure recognition of the Irish Republic from the government of the U.S., to float a Dáil Éireann External Loan and to gain for Ireland's claim worldwide publicity. If he had any doubt about the matter, the delegates told him he was the only man who could carry this programme to success.

In the second week of June 1919, Dev arrived in the U.S. Outwitting the British surveillance, he had travelled in the furnace room of a British boat under the guise of a stoker. His appearance on the American scene was a terrific sensation. Apart from the Irish who would have taken him to their hearts in any case, he was, in the eyes of Americans, a romantic figure, the last surviving Commandant of the Dublin Rising, a man who had been saved from the firing squad by a hair's breadth, one who had made a sensational escape from a British prison to become President not merely of a newly arisen European republic, but of a land which most Americans, Irish or otherwise, regarded with affection. It was no small wonder that he at once captured the heart of the American people. His tour of the Northern States and his subsequent tour of the Southern States clearly showed that the American people were wholeheartedly with him in his crusade for his people. City after city bestowed on him its freedom and in State after State he addressed the legislature. It was clear that if the decision had rested in the hands of the American people, he would have won outright all his demands. No European crowned head and no American of his day ever attracted such crowds or won such adulation.

All of this adulation would have turned the head of a lesser man, but not his. He never forgot that back home his people were under the rule of an alien tyranny and that his mission was intended to end that alien tyranny for all time. It might be a consolation for him to know that the external loan that he had floated for five million dollars was so successful that the Dáil gave him permission to extend the limit to fifteen million dollars.

But there was a fly in the ointment and it was a very big fly.

Before Dev went to America, Liam Mellowes had arrived there after the Rising. He found, as Dr. Pat McCartan found when he arrived later, that the intrusion of such people as him on the American scene was resented by the hitherto leaders of Irish–American opinion. These leaders consisted of two men. One was John Devoy, a man who had been born in Kildare and who had served a prison sentence in England in Fenian times. He was the leader of Clann na Gael, the American counterpart of the I.R.B., and the editor of the *Gaelic American*. He was an honest and sincere man, but by 1919 he had become completely deaf and he was entirely under the sway of Dan Cohalan, a judge of the Supreme Court of the State of New York.

For years these two men had been in control of the Irish vote in New York and a great many other States in the Northeast and the Middle west. Normally this vote was reckoned to be in the Democratic camp, but it happened that Cohalan had had a bitter quarrel with Woodrow Wilson on the occasion of the 1916 Democratic Convention. The judge was a man of violent temper, autocratic and arrogant to an extraordinary degree. He was fond of saying, with perfect truth, that he was one hundred per cent American and that America held his first allegiance. He was against the League of Nations because it involved foreign entanglements. He had embarked on a crusade to thwart President Wilson and to sabotage the President's pet project, the League of Nations. How this formidable man came to include de Valera in his crusade of destruction, I shall tell.

SEVEN

The Friends of Irish Freedom had raised over a million dollars as an Irish Victory Fund. Joe McGarrity of Philadelphia held that this money should be given to the Irish government to finance the struggle. Cohalan and Devoy maintained that it should be held in America and used as the Clan decided, but notably to defeat the League of Nations proposal. This issue had split the Clan itself before Dev ever arrived on the scene. At his first meeting with Cohalan, Dev listened patiently to all the judge had to say as he laid down the law as to what should and should not be done. To the judge's surprise this young man, completely unfamiliar with American politics and, indeed, with little experience with any politics at all, said politely but very definitely, that he was not opposed to the League, that indeed he was in favour of a League of Nations that would be based on self-determination, that he hoped that America would be a member of such a League and that Ireland would be admitted thereto. His objection was only to Clause 10 of the League Covenant which, if passed unaltered, would leave Ireland still in England's grasp.

Cohalan adopted new tactics. He held a private meeting in the Waldorf Hotel which he invited Dev to attend. The meeting was packed with a small selected group of Clan leaders, but there were present a few independent-minded people like Judge Goff, Robert Ford, and Michael J. Ryan of Philadelphia. Dev brought with him Harry Boland, Dr. McCartan, and Liam Mellowes. The purpose of the meeting was to persuade Dev from pursuing the ruinous course of trying to float a Dáil Éireann Loan in the United States. Led by Cohalan, speaker after speaker, many of them sincerely believing what they said, pointed out that the project was illegal and impracticable and that it would end in failure and disaster. They would give Dev a quarter of a million dollars from the Victory Fund if he would give up the project and return to Ireland. Diarmuid Lynch, an old personal friend of his, made an emotional appeal to Dev to accept the offer and even Michael J. Ryan, a reliable friend, added his voice to the appeal.

Dev, however, was adamant. "I have," he said, "a mandate from my people, and I intend to go ahead, whether I succeed or fail."

Thereafter Cohalan and Devoy placed every possible obstacle in Dev's path. It is true that in pursuing the vendetta against him, they lost many of their own supporters and it is also true that the organisation which Dev set up, the American Association for the Recognition of the Irish Republic, enrolled five or six members for the one that had belonged to the Friends of Irish Freedom, but, at the same time, the Cohalan-Devoy clique were in a position to do great harm. Dev gave an interview to the New York representative of the Westminster *Gazette* in which he replied to the argument that a free Ireland would be a menace to British security. Dev said that if such fears were real, there was nothing to prevent Britain from safeguarding itself by stipulating that Ireland would never permit any foreign power to use Irish territory for an attack on Britain, as the U.S. had done in the case of Cuba.

Devoy in the *Gaelic American* seized on this interview to embark on an open attack on the Irish President. He was accused of selling out the Republic. As a matter of fact, there was nothing in the interview to conflict with Dev's previous statement that a free Ireland would never allow Irish territory to be used as a base for an attack on Britain.The furore caused, not by the interview, but by the Devoy attack crossed the Atlantic and there was consternation and dismay in Ireland. We all knew that any suggestion of letting down the Republic would have brought a passionate protest from Mellowes. In

London, where Griffith had gone to attend a public meeting, he gave an interview in the course of which he, in the name of Dáil Éireann, strongly supported Dev's stand. On his return from London, Griffith, speaking of Cohalan and Devoy, said to me, "Their action is nothing short of high treason."

Cohalan's savage venom against Dev carried him further. The latter had hoped to get from both the Democratic and the Republican Conventions, held prior to the 1920 Presidential Election, a platform plank of recognition of the Irish Republic. His friends submitted a resolution to that effect to the Republican Convention held in Chicago on 9 June 1920. Dev had tried to get Cohalan to meet him so that they could present a united Irish front at the Convention, but the judge refused to see him. Dev's resolution was rejected in favour of a wishy-washy one which merely expressed sympathy with Ireland's aspirations. The latter had been submitted by the Cohalan camp. At the Democratic National Convention held in San Francisco later the evidence of disunity shown in Chicago had the inevitable result. The resolution for recognition was defeated, but only by a narrow margin.

The Senate of the United States, however, had already, while rejecting the Covenant of the League of Nations, ratified the Peace Treaty with Germany, with the following telling reservation:

> In consenting to the ratification of the Treaty with Germany, the United States adheres to the principle of self determination and the resolution of sympathy with the expectations of the Irish people for a government of their own choice, adopted by the Senate on the 6 June 1919, and declares that when such government is attained by Ireland, a consummation it is hoped is at hand, it should promptly be admitted as a member of the League of Nations.

De Valera cabled to Griffith, " A Te Deum should be sung throughout all Ireland."

Cohalan's fanaticism had led him to organise a secret meeting for the purpose of driving Dev from the U.S. He had a goodly body of supporters who foregathered one evening in the Park Avenue Hotel in New York City. Dev was billed to speak in Chicago the same night, so his absence was assured. But he had not gone to Chicago. Harry Boland had discovered the plot and Dev had remained in New York. Cohalan opened the meeting by launching into a bitter and biased attack on Dev. His charges grew so outrageous that Joe McGarrity, who had not been invited to the meeting, stood up and said that, in all fairness, de Valera should be given a hearing. Someone said that Dev was in Chicago. "He is not," said Joe. "He is here in New York," and he insisted on being allowed to phone for Dev. When the latter appeared with Harry Boland there was consternation. Dev addressed the gathering, explaining the purpose of his mission and his responsibility to the government of the Republic and the people of Ireland. He said he had been careful at all times never to interfere in American affairs and charged that the meeting had been called by Cohalan and Devoy for the purpose of driving him from America. When this was denied, he produced a letter showing that the conspiracy was six months old. In the uproar that followed, Judge Goff called on Cohalan to apologise to Dev and the latter did so and offered Dev his hand, which was accepted. The meeting ended when Bishop Turner called on the assembly to kneel down and say a prayer.

Towards the end of the year Dev decided that he could do no more in the U.S. He had not succeeded in getting recognition for the Republic, but he had made known to millions of Americans the truth about the Irish cause. He had founded a great Irish-American organisation and he had raised millions of dollars for the cause. He had, too, by his own unfailing courtesy and dignified bearing, placed the name of Ireland on a higher plane than it had ever occupied in America hitherto.

The arrest of Arthur Griffith and the hint that there were peace feelers helped to make up his mind. He began to make plans for his return. On Christmas Day 1920, he arrived in Ireland. Again he had crossed the Atlantic on a British ship, the S.S. *Celtic*. The British secret service men in New York had missed him and it was presumed he was on the high seas. The ship was searched, but in vain. He managed to get ashore in sailor's garb with the help of the Liverpool Irish sailors led by a man named Downes who had been a schoolboy friend of my father's.

EIGHT

I saw Dev the night after he got back from America at Christmas 1920. The courier who brought me the message had me memorise the address of the rendezvous so that nothing would be committed to writing. I cycled from the vicinity of Raheny through side streets and byways so as to avoid the wary touts and military patrols. I found Dev in a comfortable house, standing on its own ground behind a high hedge fronting Merrion Strand Road.

Years later, I heard a loud-mouthed and ignorant orator proclaim from a platform in Middle Abbey Street that Dev had ducked out during the Black and Tan terror, while others had remained to take the rap. Actually, Dev came back from America when the terror was at its height. In December 1920, no house throughout the length and breadth of Ireland was safe from the night raids of the Black and Tans and the Auxiliaries. They came usually after midnight and usually on padded soles to conceal their approach. Without warning, they would smash down the doors of a dwelling house with an axe. They maltreated the woman of the house, terrorised the children, and took the men away, if they did not murder them on the spot. During the daytime the foot patrols, backed by Crossley tenders or armoured cars, appeared here and there on the streets holding up, searching, and questioning every citizen. Assuredly the winter of 1920–1921 was no time for anyone who had a choice to visit Ireland.

Throughout the country the terror was in full swing. The British forces, urged on by bloodthirsty speeches from Lloyd

George and Birkenhead, were engaged in a systematic campaign designed to break the spirit of the people. They concentrated on the destruction of such industries as were the mainstay of the economic life of the country, such as creameries and bacon factories, which were ruthlessly destroyed.

At Christmas 1920, it was only a few weeks since the sack of Balbriggon and the burning of Cork City, the massacre at Croke Park, the brutal murder of Dick McKee, Peader Clancy and Conor Clune in Dublin Castle, the death of Terence MacSwiney in Brixton Jail, the murder of Father Griffin in Galway, and the torture and hanging of the eighteen-year-old boy, Kevin Barry, in Mountjoy Jail. After the murder of Tomas MacCurtain, the Lord Mayor of Cork, in the presence of his wife and children, the coroner's jury returned a verdict of murder against Lloyd George, Lord French and Ian McPherson.

Thereafter the British authorities decided there should be no more inquests.

This was the political atmosphere in Ireland when Dev decided to return during Christmas 1920. I found him relaxed and confident, but eager for news—at least, not for news, for he was already well-informed—but for my picture of the Irish scene. What did I think of the morale of the people? I told him quite frankly that there had been a few disturbing incidents, but that the people as a whole had not been adversely affected. There had been wide publicity of the fact that the Galway County Council had passed a resolution calling for peace, and of Father O'Flanagan's peace telegram to Lloyd George, and of the defection of a T.D. who represented Wicklow.

I was able to assure him that the resolution of the Galway County Council had been passed by a small number of councillors. I think the figure was six out of a total membership of thirty-two; that Father O'Flanagan had sent his telegram to Lloyd George without consulting anyone and that he was now very sorry he had done so, and that the Wicklow T.D. had always been regarded as a weak sister and that he amounted to nothing at all.

In a different category, however, was the case of Dr. Fogarty, the Bishop of Killaloe. The Bishop had been one of our strongest and most outspoken champions, but he had cracked up when the Black and Tans invaded his palace, intending to take his life. An emissary from Dublin Castle had warned the Bishop in time and he got away and hastened to Dublin. Griffith and I saw him in the Gresham Hotel. We found him a very chastened man. He told us that things had gone too far, that the morale of the people was cracking under the terror, and that if the tension was not eased, the people would desert Sinn Féin and transfer allegiance to the Irish Parliamentary Party.

I told Dev that A.G. was aghast at the Bishop's *volte face* and that when we came away from the interview, Griffith asked me what I thought. I replied that it was evident that the Castle—I had no doubt then or since that the whole thing was staged—had put the fear of God into his Lordship. "I quite agree," said Griffith, "it is quite clear that we cannot rely on the like of him." Apart from this, I was able to assure Dev that I had seen A.G. the day before he was arrested and that though he hated the bloodshed, and that indeed he abhorred some of the activities of the Volunteers, such as that of Bloody Sunday morning, he was was as solid against capitulation as were any of the rest of us.

Dev asked me about the activities of Sir Horace Plunkett's group and I was surprised to learn that these had attracted far more attention in America than they had at home. I told him that Captain Henry Harrison, who was supported by Sir Horace, A.E., Captain Stephen Gwynn and others, had set up an office in Dawson Street to promote a settlement based on Dominion Home Rule. Captain Harrison had consulted me on the project and I had told him that such activities as his were merely encouraging Lloyd George to think that the Republican front might be broken and that, in effect, they were prolonging the agony.

Dev deplored the fact that there was no machinery by which the American organisation could obtain quick and accurate information about the day to day events in Ireland.

For instance, the killing of the nineteen British spies on the morning of Bloody Sunday had been reported in the American Press as the murder of so many British army ex-officers in their homes in the presence of their wives. Our American friends had no means of knowing that these men were carefully selected members of a murder gang who had been sent over from England for the express purpose of murdering the chiefs of the I.R.A.

I told Dev that there might be an improvement in the matter of keeping our friends abroad well informed. I had just made an arrangement with the Dublin agents of two American firms by which I was enabled to use their cable code services.

Dev said there was one matter which had been troubling him for a long time. The Dáil had never taken responsibility for the activities of the Volunteers. The fighting men were being pictured by the British news agencies, which had the ear of the world, as a bunch of thugs and terrorists and murderers.

"I intend," he said, "to have this matter put right. I think the Cabinet should issue a clear and unequivocal statement to the effect that the Volunteers constitute the Army of the Republic and that their activities here have the full sanction of the government."

I agreed that such a pronouncement would clear the air. We who were working in the Publicity Department of the Dáil were well aware that while we gave every day in the *Irish Bulletin* a factual account of the depredations of the British forces and of the counter-measures taken by the Volunteers, we had been very careful not to describe the activities of the latter as official. To tell the truth, I was a bit surprised that Dev should have taken this line, and my surprise showed that I had not yet taken the full measure of this man. It is true that he had been abroad while I had not. He had seen that the description of the activities of the Volunteers as a band of terrorists and thugs had created in the minds of outsiders a picture that was totally distorted. Lloyd George, who had at the time a tremendous reputation abroad, especially in America, had said he had "murder by the throat", meaning that he had got a stranglehold on the I.R.A. in Ireland.

The seeming repudiation of the Volunteers by the Dáil had had its origin in Soloheadbeg. On the very day the first Dáil was set up, a band of Volunteers headed by Seumas Robinson and Dan Breen had ambushed a party of the Royal Irish Constabulary conveying explosives on a Tipperary road. Two R.I.C. constables were shot dead and the Volunteers made off with the explosives and the dead men's rifles and ammunition. Griffith, who at the time was a prisoner in Gloucester Jail, said to me that this was an outlaw action and that it had not been authorised by the Dáil. Consequently, the Dáil had always veered away from taking responsibility for the activities of the Volunteers. We could take full advantage of the ground the fighting men could win for us, but we could not take responsibility for their actions.

But now, here was de Valera saying that not merely could the Dáil take responsibility for such action, but that they should noise it far and wide. The Volunteers would henceforth be the army of the Irish Republic, and everyone, friend or foe, should know it.

When I cycled back to Raheny that night, I had a new sense of exhilaration. Something missing from the Irish scene since Dev had left us had been restored.

NINE

On his return from America at Christmas 1920, Dev found that the members of the Republican cabinet were as solid as he expected on the main question that there should be no weakening in the face of British terror. Griffith was, of course, in jail and, in his absence, Collins, with his terrific drive, had become a colossal figure in the movement. Not only was he Minister for Finance, Director of Army Organisation, Director of Communications, and Director of Intelligence, but he was now the Acting President of the Republic. In the background and seldom mentioned was the fact that he had also become Chief of the Irish Republican Brotherhood, the secret organisation whose ramifications at this time embraced practically every senior officer of the Army.

I confided to Dev that there were a few of us who were uneasy about the effect that all this power would have on Mick. Dev waved my fears aside and said that, if nothing else, Mick's standing with the fighting men would keep him on the right road.

In any case, in the spring of 1921, we were so beset by the activities of the enemy that, if for no other reason, we had to stand side by side. Every day brought news of some new atrocities committed by British forces: of whole villages burnt down, of comrades tortured or murdered. Practically all the counties in the South and West were brought under martial law and the curfew hours were extended so that no one dare appear out of doors after 8 p.m., and this during the most glorious early summer we had had in years.

Dev had moved to a house in Mount Merrion Avenue in the Blackrock area and I saw him only when it was absolutely necessary. Sometimes it was on some question in connection with the Department of which I was now in charge, having been appointed Under-Secretary for Foreign Affairs. More often, I had to bring a foreign correspondent to see him. He had become cautious because of his American experience that he nearly always insisted on being supplied with a questionnaire in advance. There was one important American journalist whom he refused to see at all. Harry Boland had sent me a report to the effect that this man was a British agent. I doubted this at the time and thought that the report was based on the fact that the man's dispatches had a pro-British slant. I changed my opinion later.

Collins, unlike Dev, said he would see the man, remarking that if he was really a British agent he would find out what he was up to. To my surprise, at the interview, the reporter openly flattered Collins by paying him the most extravagant compliments and Mick swallowed them all and, indeed, he waxed eloquent under the ministrations of the visitor. However, he did take the precaution of ensuring that before any account of the interview should be published, he had to see and vet the copy.

At this time Dev was having a tough time trying to keep the peace between Brugha and Collins, on the one hand, and Stack and Collins, on the other. Both Brugha and Stack were headstrong men and when Mick reached over, as he frequently did, to interfere in their departments, Defence in the one case, and Home Affairs in the other, both of them flared up. In defence of Collins it must be said that when any of the hard-pressed loyal Volunteer officers came to Dublin to get a much-needed decision or to secure army supplies, it was Collins they all sought out, because it was only through him that they could get quick results. Mick hated delay or indecision and he never failed to say so in the most vigorous terms. His aggressive attitude antagonised many of his colleagues, but the men who were his lieutenants would take anything from him and they idolised him.

It is an unfortunate characteristic of our race that we are prone, particularly in the revolutionary movement, to form cliques which often led to factions. As early as March 1918, there were whispers that Dev was not as staunch a Republican as he might be; that he was a moderate and that he might compromise. This may have had its origin in the fact that he had refused to have anything to do with the I.R.B. It was only a murmur at first, but by 1921 it had become painfully audible to most of us who were close to headquarters.

Tom Barry in his splendid book, *Guerilla Days in Ireland*, tells how he was summoned from West Cork to have an interview with de Valera in Dublin in May 1921. He had never met Dev and he was warned by certain people in Dublin that he was going to meet a cold, austere puritan, who was icily aloof from the people, a man who was anxious to stop the fight and who was about to accept an offer of Dominion Home Rule. Tom well describes the pleasant shock he got when he found Dev a warm, courteous, affable and likeable human being and that not merely was he not anxious to stop the fight, but that he wanted it developed. Tom says of Dev:

> He was not merely the spokesman of the people but the main architect and inspiration of victory against the British. If the finest years of our long and chequered struggle for freedom were those from 1916 to 1921, when the unity, self-respect, intelligence, and courage of the Irish people reached the heights, then too was the nation blessed with this man's leadership which was worthy of a risen people.

One aspect of the struggle which occupied a great deal of Dev's mind at this time was that since the visit of Archbishop Clune in December 1920 there had been many other peace feelers emanating from England. Growing resentment in America at the savage treatment of the Irish people was reflected in the fact that many influential English journals, led by the London *Times* and the *Manchester Guardian*, were denouncing the terrorist regime, as were also the British Labour Party, the leaders of the Protestant church and many notable British spokesmen including Asquith, Sir John Simon and others.

Day by day, it was becoming more and more obvious that Lloyd George would be forced to call a halt and seek a settlement. Dev had steadfastly refused to have anything to do with the secret talks which were being carried on. He said that if the British had anything to offer, the offer should be made openly and debated openly. In this he was adamant. At the same time, he was fully cognisant of the fact that those of his advisers who told him that no British government could, or would, agree to an absolutely independent Irish Republic on England's flank, were probably right. He set himself the task of devising a formula by which the age-long struggle for Irish freedom could be reconciled with Britain's claims.

On a memorable day in May 1921, I was in Madame O'Rahilly's house in Pembroke Park with Dev, Childers, and Collins, watching Dev draw a design with a compass. There was a very large circle within which there were five separate and independent circles. Outside the large circle there was another smaller circle having contact with it.

"There it is," said Dev, "the large circle is the British Empire. The circles within are the Dominions, Australia, New Zealand and so forth. Outside, not belonging to it but associated with it is Ireland, an independent Republic."

The scheme was a painstaking, sincere, and well-thought-out plan to reconcile the two schools of thought. Only a rare political genius could have evolved it. It was what afterwards came to be called External Association embodied in Document Number Two. It would have ensured a free and independent thirty-two county Irish Republic living in amity with Britain, beside which island we will have to exist so long as grass grows and water runs. The scheme was never given the careful consideration it merited. Dev, faced with the headlong stampede to ratify the Treaty, a step which ensured Partition and, as it was feared, Civil War, was forced to bring it before the Dáil in an effort to save the nation from disaster. In the bitter atmosphere prevailing, the scheme was torn to shreds without having been considered or even read.

If it had been adopted, there was more than a good chance that it might have saved us from the disaster that subsequently befell our nation. That was not to be so. It is a poor consolation for us to know that it was later found good enough for India, and who today will maintain that India is not free?

TEN

On 24 June 1921, Lloyd George wrote a letter to de Valera appealing for a conference between the British government and the representatives of Northern and Southern Ireland and asking him to attend such a conference in London in the company of Sir James Craig, the Premier of Northern Ireland, to explore the possibilities of a settlement.

Dev had been arrested two days before in a raid on the house at which he had been staying in Blackrock. He had been taken as a suspected felon and treated as such. Only a few weeks earlier, he and his comrades had been described by Lloyd George as "a murder gang". The British Prime Minister, boasting of the supposed successes of the Crown forces over the I.R.A., had said he had "murder by the throat". Now here was that same Prime Minister inviting Dev to sit, presumably as an equal, at a peace conference in 10 Downing Street. What had happened?

On 22 June King George V visited Belfast for the purpose of opening the Northern Parliament and he astounded his hosts by throwing aside the speech prepared for him and substituting one of his own. In this he prayed that his visit to Ireland might prove to be the first step towards the end of strife among her people whatever their race or creed. He appealed to all Irishmen to pause and stretch out the hand of forbearance and conciliation, to forgive and forget and to join in making for the land they loved a new era of peace, contentment and good will. He said that the future of Ireland lay in the hands of the Irish people themselves and prayed that the Irish people, North and South, would work together in common love for Ireland upon the sure foundation of mutual justice and respect.

Lloyd George, a quick change artist if ever there was one, seized the opportunity given him by the King's speech to disentangle himself from the net he had got into over his Irish policy. That fact that Dev's arrest coincided with the King's speech was for him a godsend. He ordered that Dev should be at once released and informed that he might expect a letter from him. Dev was as much dumbfounded by his release as were the rest of the people of Ireland, and for three days all Ireland was left guessing until the arrival of Lloyd George's letter inviting the Irish leaders to a London conference. Lloyd George cunningly based his *volte face* on the King's appeal for reconciliation.

Dev was instantly aware of the dangers in this new development. He knew that throughout the whole country the relief that the end of the reign of terror was in sight would be overwhelming. For three years the people had endured untold horrors at the hands of a merciless tyranny. Hundreds of loved one who had been killed would never return; hundreds of others would now be free for the first time in years to return to their homes. There were at the moment over forty men in the hands of the British who might be hanged if a peace solution was not found. People in thousands who had never in years had an easy night, fearing the dreaded night raids, could now for the first time sleep easily in their beds; young boys and girls, who had been afraid to walk abroad, could now bask in the June sunshine and walk when and where they pleased without fear of the dreaded armoured cars, the Crossley tenders, and the evil auxiliaries with their guns at the ready.

Dev knew all this. His people's plight had been his plight. His wife and children, whom he had seldom seen in the intervening years, had themselves undergone the same agony. They, too, had known the terror of the dark nights, the stealthy approach of uniformed and licensed murderers on padded feet, the waiting for the axe splitting the door, the dread news of the death of a loved one. All this was known to him and let no one who has not been through it belittle the ordeal our people underwent in those days.

Dev knew all this. He fully realised what a relief the lifting of the terror would be, but he never forgot that he had been given a mandate by the Irish people. He was the spearhead in the struggle to win the right of Irish people to rule their own land. On him devolved the duty of seeing that the alien rule under which his people laboured should now be ended once and for all. He feared that with the easing of the terror there would be a softening of the nation's determination and in a public declaration he warned against this. He said that this easement was not a victory, but a challenge. The people should be ready to resume the fight with all its rigours if such became necessary.

He himself had resolved to find a solution which would end this ancient struggle and he believed it could be done.

When he read Lloyd George's letter he saw at once that it was not what it purported to be—an honest approach to the solution of the problem. It involved, in the first place, the tacit acceptance of Ireland's inclusion in the Empire, the recognition of the partition of the country, and the implied denial of Dev's own position as the elected head of the Irish nation. Lloyd George's letter was the beginning of a correspondence which lasted through all of fourteen agonising weeks. After the lapse of 38 years, I have gone through the whole of this correspondence from beginning to end and I can only marvel at the foresight, the fortitude and the astuteness shown by de Valera in dealing with the duplicity that was Lloyd George's second nature.

Dev clearly saw the implications contained in Lloyd George's first letter and cleverly side-stepped them. He invited Sir James Craig and the leaders of the Southern Unionists in Dublin in order to make clear the fact that he was spokesman for all Ireland. Craig ignored the invitation, but the Southern Unionists attended and Dev thereupon accepted Lloyd George's invitation, having first successfully insisted that there should be a truce.

It is a great pity that there exists no shorthand report of the first meeting between Dev and Lloyd George. There is no doubt but that the Welsh wizard was at his best as he discussed the relative merits of the Welsh and Irish languages. The meeting lasted for three hours and ended amicably. It had been arranged that Dev was to await the British terms for a settlement, and amongst the members of the Irish team there was a feeling of complacency. A couple of days ensued before the British terms were delivered to Dev. They were so outrageous that he was flabbergasted. It was clear that Lloyd George had vastly underrated his man. Dev saw the Prime Minister as soon as he could and told him that the terms were completely unacceptable and that not merely did he reject them but that he would not even bring them back to Ireland for consideration. He returned to Ireland that night.

He was not downhearted. He knew that the first honours of the peace table encounter were his. His people were standing firm and be believed that they would continue to do so. His knowledge of Irish history told him that in the past Ireland had been defeated not because the people failed their leaders in the hours of crisis, but because the leaders had failed the people. Moreover, he was astute enough to know that in all such negotiations it was traditional for the British to demand far more than they were likely to obtain so that at a crucial point in the negotiations they could gain an advantage by yielding on a trivial point previously agreed on amongst themselves. An instance of this, which would be amusing if it were not set in such a potentially tragic atmosphere, is given by Frank Pakenham in his book, *Peace by Ordeal*. Childers had drawn up a masterly memorandum which showed that acceptance of the Crown would have a far different meaning in Ireland than it would in the case of Canada. In law Canada was a subordinate dependency, whereas in fact she had a status equal to that of Great Britain. By law the British Parliament could make laws for Canada, whereas in fact Canada alone could legislate for Canada. Because, however, of the proximity of Ireland to Britain if for no other reason, the law for Ireland would be the fact and the nominal subordination would be real. For four days the delegates had mulled over this clause about the Crown, and when the delegates next faced Lloyd George they were prepared to debate the question for days on end if necessary. The discussion, however, had lasted only a short while when, as Pakenham said, "the British hold on the rope loosened and the Irish went sprawling on their backs". They were told that they could insert in the Treaty "any phrase they liked which would ensure that the position of the Crown in Ireland should be no more in practice than it was in Canada or in any other Dominion."

Dev seemed to sense in advance that the British would pursue such tactics as this. Unlike Lloyd George, his attitude was perfectly straight and honest from the start. He really wanted a final settlement to the age-long quarrel, a settlement that would enable his country and her people to live in amity with the neighbouring island and to advance her own manifest destiny in peace.

And he would have done so if he had not been let down by men of lesser vision.

ELEVEN

Number Ten Downing Street has a tradition extending back for hundreds of years. From its august precincts the rulers of the British Empire had been accustomed to deliver edicts which involved the lives and fortunes of countless generations of less fortunate people than those of England. A word from Number Ten could dispose of the fate of millions of people in Africa and Asia and of "the lesser breeds without the law" in far off lands and, indeed, this was the case in countries nearer home until recent times.

Lloyd George who, in his day, was one of the foremost of liberals, who, indeed, stood up against the English Tories in the Boer War and who in his struggle against that iniquitous war on one occasion had had his life saved from an English mob by the Irish in an English city, might have been expected to understand the Irish question. But now he was the British Prime Minister. He was His Majesty's First Minister, ruling the greatest empire on earth. The country solicitor from Wales had become the man who held dominion over palm and pine. He was now charged with a commission. He was to bring the Irish to heel. He was faced with the task of solving a problem which had defied the ingenuity of the greatest of British statesmen for two or three hundred years, that of getting the Irish to conform, of getting those recalcitrant Irish to march in step with a British people who had conquered the world. Were they to be hampered by an Ireland that had been off and on in rebellion for nearly two hundred years? Lloyd George knew that this rebellious Ireland had a vast but unknown reservoir of strength from her sons and daughters overseas and that these would have to be placated by any offer he could make to the Irish at home. He knew, too, that in the offer he could make he would have to ensure his own position as head of a British coalition government, which included such Tories as Birkenhead and Chamberlain and such a newly converted Tory as Winston Churchill.

All of this must be taken into account when we consider the terms offered by Lloyd George in his letter to Dev which was delivered on 20 July 1921. The terms completely ignored the principle of self-determination. Ireland was invited to take her place in the great association of free nations over which His Majesty reigned. Under the new regime Ireland would have free autonomy in taxation, finance, and education, but there was to be free trade between the two countries. England was to have such naval and air facilities in Ireland as she deemed necessary. Ireland was to contribute in proportion to her wealth to the cost of Britain's forces and voluntary recruiting to those forces should be permitted. Ireland should recognise the existing powers and privileges of the Parliament of Northern Ireland.

Dev had promised Lloyd George a considered reply to these proposals and he dispatched this on 10 August. In the course of it he said:

> Ireland's right to choose for herself the path she shall take to realise her own destiny must be accepted as indefeasible. It is a right that . . . will not be surrendered. We cannot propose to abrogate or impair it, nor can Britain or any other foreign state or group of states legitimately claim to interfere with its exercise in order to serve their own special interests.

The exchange of letters lasted until the end of September and throughout the whole period Dev managed to evade the many pitfalls the British Prime Minister had laid for him. As Dorothy Macardle says,

> the Republic had been safeguarded from compromise and the people from aggression. When the Delegation went to London they were

uncommitted to anything save "to ascertain how the association of Ireland with the community of nations known as the British Empire may best be reconciled with Irish national aspirations."

The bitterly anti-Irish *Morning Post* commented, "De Valera . . . will come to the Conference as one who has already gained his point. Even the elementary condition that he should acknowledge the sovereignty of the Crown has been waived."

The question has often been asked, "Why did de Valera himself not go to London?" The simple answer is that he wanted to provide the Delegation with a ready way to evade any trap the British might set for them. Apart from the generally accepted belief that the British were very adroit at the conference table, Dev had faced Lloyd George and knew what a slippery customer he was. If at any time the delegates were in a tight corner, they could always plead that they had to consult Dublin.

The delegates had given an undertaking that before signing any treaty, the complete text would be submitted to Dublin and the reply awaited. Notwithstanding this, they signed a treaty which had not been submitted to Dublin and which split Ireland from end to end. Why had this come about? The story is a terrible one as anyone who has read Frank Pakenham's book, *Peace by Ordeal*, knows. The negotiations had lasted for over eight weeks and culminated in three days during which the delegates were worn out by long discussions and by travel. At 2.15 on the morning of 6 December, Lloyd George threatened immediate and terrible war if all five delegates did not sign the treaty then and there without recourse to Dublin.

Dev had made one miscalculation. It was one anyone would have made. He did not know that from the start of the peace negotiations certain of the Irish army chiefs had lost faith in their ability to attain what they mistakenly thought was the objective of the fight. After nearly three years of relying on the gun, they had come to the conclusion that they were expected to drive the British out by force and they could not do that. Actually, their task was to make British government in Ireland impossible. In this they had succeeded. In fact the real objective of the fight had been won when certain military chiefs thought it had been lost. There was another factor which played its part in the disaster. Few people outside the secret organisation at the time were aware that the attitude of the I.R.B. could be expressed in the phrase "Get the British out, give us the guns, and we'll do the rest."

The frame of mind behind this phrase was characteristic of the mentality of the I.R.B. or at least certain leaders of that organisation. At one time a leader of the movement was, in effect, put on trial because he participated in a civic welcome to a British monarch who visited Ireland. He maintained that though he held no allegiance to the British monarch, he was justified in his action because any duplicity on the part of an Irishman was justified vis à vis Great Britain. He was thrown out, but his contention that any duplicity was justified was shared by many people in the secret movement. The contention was that England never failed to practise such dubious means of attaining her ends and why should not we.

Few of us in the rank and file shared a belief in such devious ways and, indeed, it is an outstanding characteristic of the Irishman that no matter what, he will stand over his word or his signature. When I was in America, I found that this was recognised as almost a truism. The Irishman in America may be a crook, or he may belong to, say, a Tammany organisation, but he will never double-cross a partner, whether the partnership be good or bad. If he gives his word, he will stand by it be the consequences what they may.

Lloyd George knew this. That was why he insisted that the delegates sign their names to the document in the early hours of 6 December 1921.

TWELVE

From the moment the vote on the Treaty was taken, Eamon de Valera set himself the task of trying to repair the damage done. All through the Dáil debates he was foremost amongst those deputies who had refrained from indulging in personalities. It is held to be universally true that of all quarrels, a family quarrel is the most bitter and any Irishman today reading the record of those debates, after 37 years, must feel a sense of humiliation at the bitter jibes which were hurled from one side or the other. While holding steadfast to his belief that the Treaty was a betrayal of the Republic, Dev was careful not to say one word that would bar the way to future collaboration with those who opposed him.

When the Dáil voted 64 to 57 to recommend the Treaty he, for the first time, showed how deeply he was affected. He stood up to make a plea for discipline. He said, "We have had four years of magnificent discipline in our nation. The world is looking at us now . . . ".

He sat back unable to finish his speech and buried his face in his hands. The sob he gave vent to echoed throughout the hall and, indeed, throughout the nation. The hearts of his people were with him still, but the longing for peace amongst the people tired of a war in which the odds were so unequal was overwhelming. Dev knew this as well as any other man. He had himself said that it was natural that everyone would vote for the Christmas holidays. But he knew that the holiday offered, based on the Treaty, would only entail a resumption of the conflict at a later day and he still hoped that if the old comrades stood together once more they could achieve peace by presenting a united front to Britain and winning a settlement which all the Irish could honourably accept.

Any man less resolute facing the terrible odds now arrayed against him would have retired from the political scene and sought the rest he had so well earned. For a while, indeed, he thought of doing so. He had told the Dáil that he was sick and tired of the politics he had seen during the Treaty debates. But the Republic had not yet been disestablished and he hoped the people would reverse the decision.

All through the spring and summer he sought to bring the rival forces together and when he finally persuaded Collins to sign the Collins–de Valera Pact he thought he had succeeded. The Pact, if it had been carried out, would have enabled both sides to work in harmony for the attainment of national ideals. Collins hailed the Pact and said it would bring stable conditions to the country and if those stable conditions were not more vulnerable than any other agreement, well then, they must face what those stable conditions enabled them to face. This meant, if anything, that reconciliation amongst the Republicans was more important than the Treaty.

The country rejoiced but everyone apparently reckoned without the British leaders who were furious over the Pact. Collins was summoned to London and when he returned he made a speech in Cork in which he repudiated the Pact, only five days after he had made a public appeal in support of it. Dev read the speech in the newspapers and not merely was he lost in dismay but he was completely bewildered at this turn of events. He was handicapped by the fact that he was unaware of the devious methods being employed by the Free State leaders in two important matters. One of these concerned the draft constitution being drawn up by the Provisional government and the other the machinations of the I.R.B.

It had been promised that the Constitution would contain no clause repugnant to the continuance of the Republic and that it would be published before the General Election was held, so that the people could judge. The fact was kept secret that when Griffith brought the draft to London it was contemptuously rejected by the British ministers and another draft substituted, which contained a dozen clauses repugnant to the maintenance of the Republic. It vested the executive authority in the British monarch, who had the power of veto over all Irish legislation; no member of the Oireachtas could take his seat until he had taken an oath of allegiance; there was to be a Governor General, the representative of the King, and he was to summon and dissolve parliament, appoint ministers and sign acts of parliament; the parliament could vote no money for any purpose not recommended by him; he was to appoint the judges of all the courts. It was provided that appeal could be made from the Irish Supreme Court to the King's Privy Council.

This document was withheld from publication until the morning of the election and it was clear that only a small percentage of the voters could have read it before they voted. The result of the election was that of the 128 seats, 94 were won by the Panel candidates, of whom 58 were pro-Treaty and 36 anti-Treaty. As the 17 Labour candidates returned all supported the Pact, it was a clear win for the Pact, but the Free State party claimed that it was a victory for the Treaty and proceeded to act accordingly. The Pact had provided that there should be a Coalition ministry consisting of five pro-Treaty and four anti-Treaty members. After the election no Republican was invited to join the ministry.

The other vital circumstance of which Dev was unaware was that the I.R.B. had planned the assassination of Sir Henry Wilson and that Collins was party to the plan of sending an armed expedition against North-east Ulster. The fact was that Collins had agreed with Craig to end the Belfast boycott in the hope that the merciless pogrom of nationalists in Belfast, Derry and other northern cities would be brought to an end. Instead, however, the pogroms continued and, indeed, were intensified. Collins agreed that the expedition to the North should be a joint one between the Free State G.H.Q. and the Republican Army H.Q. in the Four Courts. An exchange of rifles was effected between Beggars Bush, the Free State Army H.Q., and the Four Courts Garrison, so that the guns which the British had handed over to the Free State forces would not be used in the attack on the North. The Free State army leaders connived at the occupation of the Four Courts, saying that so long as Republicans held the Four Courts, the attack on the North would be attributed to them.

However, on 22 June, Sir Henry Wilson was shot dead in London. No Irish nationalist mourned his death for he had shown himself to be an implacable enemy of the country of his birth. Dev was asked for a statement. He said that the killing of a human being was an awful act, but as awful when the victim was a humble worker as when the victim was placed in the seats of the mighty. It was characteristic of our hypocritical civilisation that it was in the latter case only we were to express our condemnation. He did not know why the deed was done, but he did know that life had been made a hell for the nationalist minority in Belfast and its neighbourhood for the past couple of years. "I do not approve," he said, "but I must not pretend to misunderstand."

The British government affected to believe that the deed was the work of the Republicans in the Four Courts, though even then they knew that Wilson's death had been ordained by the I.R.B., which was controlled by Collins. They ordered Collins to attack the Four Courts. On the morning of 28 June 1922, de Valera heard the death knell of his hopes for unity and peace, the noise of the guns bombarding the Four Courts—British guns manned by Irishmen. The Civil War he had dreaded and warned against and which he had striven so hard to ward off had begun.

THIRTEEN

The writer of this series of articles in the course of a long life has had occasion to remark on the power of the press. During Easter Week 1916 he had seen the effects which an English newspaper smuggled into Enniscorthy had wrought on the men in rebellion there. That paper stated the Rising was virtually over two days before the event. The account was based on half-truths and whole lies, but the men in Enniscorthy had no means of knowing this, and it had the effect of weakening the resolve of some of them to continue the fight. I mention this matter merely to point to the fact that from the moment the negotiations started in 1921, the dice were loaded against Dev so far as the press was concerned. There was not a metropolitan newspaper in Ireland on his side. They were all against him, covertly during the negotiations and openly after the Treaty debates began. Day after day loaded editorials denounced him as a warmonger, a quibbler, and a dangerous demagogue. His every speech was attacked and misrepresented.

Not one of those metropolitan dailies had ever espoused the cause of the Republic. Even after the 1918 elections when it was crystal clear that 75 per cent of the people supported the stand made by the heroes of 1916, even after the establishment of Dáil Éireann in 1919, there was not a single metropolitan daily which gave wholehearted, or even half-hearted support to the Republican cause. After the Treaty had been signed in London and when de Valera denounced it because its terms were "in violent conflict with the wishes of the majority of this nation as freely expressed in successive elections during the past three years", they embarked on a campaign of misrepresentation and abuse such as I have never known. Day after day they reviled the man whom they knew to be the spearhead of those who opposed national surrender.

The reason I dwell on this is because during the period when Dev was fighting this uphill battle to save not merely the honour of the nation, but also to ward off the catastrophe he saw ahead, which was civil war, he was tripped up at every turn by a hostile press. When he pointed out, quite truly, that acceptance of the Treaty would lead inevitably to civil war, he was actually accused of fomenting civil war. This malignant campaign succeeded. When the guns at last spoke and the English warlords were rejoicing over the fact that at their bidding the civil war was being fought "with an economy of English lives", the label, "the man who caused the civil war" was pinned on Dev and it stayed there a long time.

Even after the Four Courts was attacked he still strove for peace, but his appeal to the Free State leaders went unanswered. When Dublin had fallen and I joined him in Clonmel, he was pleading with Liam Lynch to open negotiations with Collins while the Republicans still had a bargaining position—the fact that they held that portion of the country south of a line from Limerick to Wexford. He failed in his efforts for peace, but he loyally stayed by his comrades in the field and after the fall of Fermoy he shared their hardships in the guerilla war which followed. They were hunted night and day by an Irish army which gained ever-increasing strength from the copious military supplies coming from the enemies of the Irish nation. It was a bitter trial, but he never lost heart. When his comrade Liam Lynch was killed in the mountains of Tipperary, he wrote an address to the army in which he said they had flung themselves across the stampede of a nation, but it was better to die as Liam had died than to live as slaves. He said, "Your cause is immortal; weariness from the exacting struggle, false teachers, temporary losses and defeats may defer, but cannot prevail against the ultimate triumph."

The phrase "stampede of a nation" was no hyperbole. North, south, east and west, people were crying out for peace.

They were dead tired of war. They were exhausted in bone and sinew, in body and spirit. They longed for the time when they could resume the normal conditions of life. They saw no chance of victory for the nation in a continuance of a war which now saw on one side scattered bands of Republicans in the hills, ill clad and ill equipped, and on the other, a well-equipped army housed in barracks in every stronghold in the country. The Free State government had established a police force, a judiciary system, and a civil service.

Moreover there were tens of thousands of Republicans in the jails and the ghastly execution of Republican prisoners continued with sickening regularity. Dev, with all his powers of persuasion, had failed to get the Republican army leaders to agree to a cessation of hostilities and he did not succeed until 30 April 1923, when Frank Aiken, who had succeeded Liam Lynch as Chief of Staff, and Dev issued a joint statement ordering a ceasefire.

There was no reason in the world why Dev should not have been as exhausted as were the people generally. He had been in the thick of the trouble for seven strenuous years. Indeed, he had borne the brunt of it more than any man in Ireland. When he joined the Irish Volunteers in 1913, he shared in the exaltation of a new Ireland, disciplined and in arms. He had led the most brilliant fight in the Easter Week Rising. He had been beaten in that fight, but one has only to look at the famous picture of him when he was under arrest after the battle of Mount Street Bridge, to see that he was undefeated and, indeed, unconquerable. He had sojourned in the grimy prisons of England, garbed as a convict, and he had emerged to be greeted by the enthusiastic hosts of a newly awakened nation which with unerring judgment placed him at its head. He had met and tangled with the most astute politicians which England seems to breed more than any other race, and he had not succumbed to their wiles or threats.

He had seen his hopes blasted by the desertion of small men who thought they were wiser than he was. How small those men were compared to him! Smaller indeed than the pygmies who brought Parnell down at the bidding of the British.

He had gone through the torture of a war of brothers, a war his sage advice would have headed off if his hearers had only listened. With heartbreak he had seen old comrades on either side killed in that awful conflict, and he, a hunted man, had tramped the lonely hills with the last remnants of the tattered army that had thrown itself into the fray in the heroic effort to halt the stampede of a nation.

This indomitable man, still undismayed and still refusing to accept defeat, believed that the cause he stood for was destined for ultimate triumph. He knew in his heart that it could not be in vain that, in spite of bloody defeats, generation after generation of his people had answered the call of a free Ireland. Victory had been almost within his grasp in 1921. Maybe he could achieve it yet.

He was in hiding in Dublin when he again approached the Free State leaders. He wanted them to at least leave the way open so that all parties in the nation could march together, shoulder to shoulder. His overtures were met by sneers, cynicism and studied insults. The Free State government would not remove the oath of allegiance which debarred the Republican T.D.s from entering the Dáil. Instead, they arrested him when he went to Ennis to address his constituents in the 1923 election. They kept him in jail for a year, but, meanwhile, the splendid people of Clare had elected him with a vote of 17,000, more than twice that given the most formidable opponent the Free State people could put up against him, Dr. Eoin McNeill. Moreover, the overall returns of the election gave a faint indication that the Free State party were losing popular support, while the Republicans were gaining it. This result was the first ray of hope in a long time, but it showed that the tide was turning in favour of the Republican cause.

Dev had to wait, however, for another nine years before he could put his hand on the tiller again and when he did so he was only two weeks in office when he abolished the hated oath of allegiance which the Free State leaders said could not be altered by a comma. The British ministers ranted and raged, but Dev stood firm and let them rant and rage. All Ireland rejoiced. Here was their old hero back again, the man who could stand up to the British in the way they wanted their leaders to do.

FOURTEEN

Before he took office in 1932, de Valera had been a witness to the shameful spectacle of the small men who ruled the state as they bowed their heads year after year to the British demands. Under their rule even the meagre measure of freedom allotted to Ireland under the Treaty became more and more meagre. Whenever there was a dispute over any clause of the Treaty, the Free State ministers were called to London and, as one writer of the period put it, the Irish people shivered whenever they went because it foreshadowed another surrender of Ireland's rights.

The first major surrender was over the question of the Boundary. Article 12 of the Treaty ordained that the Boundary Commission would rectify the border between the twenty-six counties and the six counties in the north-east by taking into account the wishes of the inhabitants in the area. On the face of it, this clearly meant that wherever in such areas the majority decided in favour of joining the Free State it would be so decided. It was clear that in such a case the counties of Tyrone and Fermanagh, South Armagh and South Down, as well as the city of Derry, in all of which areas there was a nationalist majority, would opt to join the South, and this would be easy since all of these areas adjoined the Free State territory. Lloyd George had convinced Griffith that this would happen and argued that if the Northern government was deprived of these areas it would collapse.

When the Boundary Commission met, however, it was so rigged that the decision was reached that the six counties should remain an entity. The Free State government swallowed the decision.

This was the first of a series of surrenders on the part of the Free State government. It was followed by many others. Not once did they stand up to the British. While waging a savage war against their former comrades in the I.R.A., they showed a craven subservience to the British.

What a different proposition Dev was when he came to take office! Before, however, he could take office he had to clear the decks. After the Civil War and a year in jail at the hands of the Free State government, he had come to the conclusion that if Ireland was to make any headway he would have to enter the Free State Parliament. The shameful surrender of the Dublin government on the Boundary made that step imperative. Both Griffith and Collins had assured the Dáil and the country that the findings of the Boundary Commission would result in a United Ireland. Those assurances had gone far to secure support for the Treaty. Even the *Irish Independent*, a bitter opponent of de Valera's, said of the findings of the Boundary Commission that had such an outcome been known in advance, the Treaty "would never have received five minutes' consideration in this country".

It was imperative, therefore, if only to prevent further deterioration, that he should enter the Dáil. The oath was the barrier. He announced that if the oath were removed, he would lead his party into the Dáil and since the Republican deputies now numbered 48 as against 63 for the Free State party in a house of 153 seats, it was realised that his entry might have a profound effect. The Sinn Féin Executive by a majority decided against entering the Dáil under any circumstances, and he left the organisation and founded the Fianna Fáil party which was designed, as Dev said, "to get the nation out of the paralysing Treaty dilemma". Its objects were to unite the nation by healing the wounds of the Civil War, to cut the bonds of British control as imposed by the Treaty, to rebuild the nation's structure culturally and economically and to end partition. It was to be a constitutional party eschewing physical force.

It is now thirty-three years since the Fianna Fáil organisation was started and it is perhaps as well that the younger generation should be told what the Irish government set-up was at that time. There was in the Phoenix Park a Governor General who represented the British King. He had the right to veto all legislation and to appoint all ministers and judges. The courts were subject to the British King's Privy Council. Every member of the Dáil had to take an oath of allegiance to the same king. The Irish ports at Lough Swilly, Berehaven and Cobh were occupied by British naval forces and the British could occupy any and all Irish harbours in time of war or threat of war. Finally, all civil and military aviation to and from Ireland was subject to British control.

All of those disabilities have vanished, thanks to the superb statesmanship of Eamon de Valera, but away back in 1926 there were few believed that he could attain his objective by the means he outlined, or indeed by any means. The Free State government was safely in the saddle and he was a voice crying in the wilderness. He had stated that he would enter the Dáil if the oath were removed, but the Free State leaders had no intention of accommodating him. They said that the oath could not be altered by a comma without jeopardising the Treaty.

However, a tragedy in which he had neither hand act nor part sent the Fianna Fáil party into the Dáil. Kevin O'Higgins, the strongman of the Free State party, was shot down on a Sunday morning on his way to church. To this day, no one outside the actual perpetrators of the deed knows who was responsible. He had made bitter enemies of the Republicans, but he had also taken strong measures against certain elements in the Free State army and police force.

At the time I was convinced that the authorities were puzzled and that they did not know where to look for the people responsible. They arrested and re-arrested several friends of mine who, as they well knew, could have had nothing at all to do with it. However, they introduced legislation which gave them wide powers of search and arrest, and also an act under which every candidate at parliamentary elections would be required to take the oath of allegiance before he could be nominated.

Dev now had to make up his mind. His party would be debarred even from contesting elections in the future unless they were prepared to take the oath. In the circumstances, he decided to take the oath, regarding it as the Free State ministers avowed it to be, "an empty formula", but he gave a solemn promise that as soon as he took office, his first act would be to abolish the oath. He was as good as his word, as usual.

He was only a few weeks in office when he decided on another step which was to have a profound effect on the future of Ireland. Before the election he had stated that if he came into office he would refuse to pay into the British Exchequer the annuities collected from the Irish farmers; he had been advised that such payments were illegal. When he told the British government that the payments were to be held in the Irish Treasury, Mr. Jimmy Thomas, the British Dominions Secretary, hurried over to Dublin. Mr. Thomas had been an excellent Trade Union official, but he was a poor diplomat. His hearty, happy-go-lucky manner got him nowhere with Dev who, however, said that he was willing to have the question submitted to arbitration. Mr. Thomas suggested that the arbitrators should be from within the Empire, but Dev said no. It would have to be an international tribunal. Mr. Thomas returned to London and reported to the House of Commons that Dev was an impossible man to deal with. Lloyd George agreed with Mr. Thomas and said that Mr. de Valera's attitude was that Ireland was a sovereign state which should have the same relation to Britain as Belgium had to Germany and Portugal had to Spain.

"It is," said Lloyd George, "a clear demand from which Mr. de Valera has never swerved for one day. He is that type; he will never change right to the end."

The Welsh wizard had unconsciously paid de Valera the greatest tribute of his life. The British Tories were furious and the Irish rejoiced because their champion had again proved himself more than a match for them.

The British then imposed a penal tariff on Irish cattle entering England and the Irish government, in retaliation, imposed penal tariffs on British goods entering Ireland. The ruinous economic war lasted for five years. It inflicted grievous injuries on Irish farmers and on English traders but, in the end, Ireland won. Neville Chamberlain, the British Prime Minister, came to an agreement with Dev under which Ireland was no longer to pay five million pounds a year to England but would pay a lump sum of ten million pounds. More important was a clause in the agreement that the British were to surrender the ports of Lough Swilly, Berehaven and Cobh to Ireland and their claim to facilities in Irish ports and harbours in time of war.

It was this clause which saved Ireland from being involved in the Second World War. It was de Valera's supreme achievement up to that time and his opponents have never been generous enough to give him for it the credit which is his due.

FIFTEEN

Those who did not live during the Twenties cannot realise the degree of hostility encountered by de Valera during and after the Civil War. Ministers of State had openly boasted that he would be driven out of political life for ever. There were actually two attempts made to set up a Fascist State which had for one of their objects that purpose. The first of these which was organised by a number of Free State army officers was squelched by the intervention of certain members of the former government. The second, however, had the blessings of the whole Free State party and, for some time, looked like a real menace to the very foundation of the state.

As a result of the general election in the spring of 1932, Dev emerged leading the strongest party and though not having a majority of seats in the Dáil, he decided to take office with the tacit support of the Labour Party.

On the eve of the assembling of the Dáil, a number of Free State officers hurried to Dublin with the idea of taking over Government Buildings, setting up a military dictatorship and imprisoning all who stood in their way, including de Valera and the Fianna Fail T.D.s, if not also the Labour T.D.s. Some of those officers had already established a name for themselves for terrorism during the Civil War, but they cannot have been very bright because they sent emissaries to the Curragh Camp with the idea of enrolling support from that quarter. They had little or no success there and one of the Free State officers who had been approached raced in to Dublin and acquainted one of the Fianna Fáil leaders of the fell design. The latter hastened to the Archbishop of Dublin, who got in touch with Mr. W.T. Cosgrave, who in turn took prompt measures and headed off the intended putsch and succeeded in doing so.

A later attempt to set up a military dictatorship met with more success and we had the extraordinary spectacle of the whole Free State party donning Blue Shirts and parading in military formation in imitation of Mussolini's Black Shirts in Italy and Hitler's Brown Shirts in Germany.

What happened was that when Dev took office in 1932 he made a rigid rule, much to the disgust of many of his hungry followers, that there should be no spoils system in the Irish Civil Service or the Army. He took the view that the Civil Service and the Army would be considered loyal servants of the State unless or until they could be proved to be otherwise. This wise and courageous decision has had a profound effect in establishing a stable condition in the Irish State. It was known at the time that the vast majority of army personnel was hostile to the Republicans and that most of the civil servants were of a like mind. Dev held that only by trusting then to remain loyal to the State, whoever was in charge, that a real democratic regime could be set up and maintained. In this his judgement has been justified.

There was one man, however, who could not be continued in office. General Eoin O'Duffy, who was a T.D. for Monaghan, had taken a leading part in the Dáil debates on behalf of the Treaty, he had been one of the most active opponents of the Republicans during the Civil War, and he was high in the counsels of the Irish Republican Brotherhood. When Dev took over, O'Duffy was the Chief of Police. It was a key position in the life of the State and Dev felt that if he remained in that position, the stability of the State would be endangered. He dismissed O'Duffy but—as his Republican critics have so often averred—more generous to his enemies than to his friends, he gave him a pension of a thousand pounds a year.

The irate general immediately embarked on a campaign. He founded what he called the League of Youth, with "a corporative state" as his objective. His adherents dressed themselves in blue shirts and blue berets, parading here and there throughout the country.

What followed is almost incredible. Mr. Cosgrave, who had hitherto led a party which had seemed to stand for something solid however shaky its foundations, abdicated in favour of General O'Duffy and handed over the sceptre to him. Even more incredible is the fact that a newly formed conservative group called the Centre Party, headed by Frank MacDermot and James Dillon, did likewise.

De Valera was sorely beset at the time. The economic war was well under way. The large ranchers were in full cry against the government because the penal tariffs exacted by the British government on cattle exported to England were injuring their business. The sons and daughters began to parade through the land dressed in blue shirts, or blue blouses, and blue berets. General O'Duffy's star seemed to be in the ascendant. His campaign throughout the country, in spite of his uninspiring leadership, was gaining recruits everywhere. He proclaimed that his object was to save the country from Communism and, strange to say, many people listened to him though everyone knew that the last country in Europe where Communism could find a foothold was Ireland.

The Blue Shirt movement, however, spread surprisingly fast and recruits were flocking to O'Duffy's side. The General, at his meetings, used Fascist symbols and gave the Fascist salute. He boasted that the Blue Shirt flag would soon by flying beside the Tricolour over Government Buildings in Merrion Street. Not only that, but the leaders of the Free State Party were proclaiming that the Black Shirts were victorious in Italy and the Brown Shirts in Germany and soon the Blue Shirts would be equally victorious in Ireland. Can anyone today believe that such people as Mr. Costello and Mr. Dillon were parties to this nonsense? But such was the fact.

It was not all nonsense, however. The country was faced with a serious menace. The Blue Shirts embarked on a militant campaign. The big farmers refused to pay their rates and the Blue Shirts in order to obstruct the officers of the law started to cut down telegraph poles, tore up railway lines, trenched roads, and felled trees.

Dev with his usual patience, tantalising at times to his supporters, saw all these things happening and finally realised that if he did not act the country was heading for another civil war, and in March 1934 he took action. He introduced a bill in the Dáil which made it an offence for anyone right or left to organise private armies. He said that the pretence that the Blue Shirts were organised to save the country from Communism was a hollow one and he was able to show from General O'Duffy's own reports to the government when he had been Chief of Police, that Communism was virtually non-existent in Ireland which, of course, everyone knew very well.

In his speech to the Dáil, Dev said:

> This country is not a natural breeding ground for communism and everybody knows it. It is opposed to our religion; it is opposed to our individualistic tendencies; it is opposed to our whole scheme of life. If there is one country in the world which is unsuitable for Communism, it is this . . . I have never stood for Communism in any form. I loathe and detest it as leading to the same sort of thing that I loathe and detest in the type of state that General O'Duffy would set up because they are both destructive of human liberty.

Concluding his speech, Dev appealed to all parties in the Dáil to join him in averting a situation which would lead to civil war, and he presented to the Dáil a picture he had brought back from America, where the bitterness of the civil war there had lasted for more than sixty years.

I have no doubt at all that if General O'Duffy had been an abler man, the menace to the infant state would have been a serious one. But, as it happened, the General proved a damp squib. He projected a march on Dublin in the manner of Mussolini's march on Rome. Dev called out the army to bar the approaches to Dublin and his faith in the army was justified. They held the approaches to Dublin and the projected march on Dublin was called off. The Blue Shirts were disbanded and General O'Duffy vanished from the political scene.

In the meantime, de Valera had become a worldwide figure. As the representative of the Irish nation, he had presided at the thirteenth session of the League of Nations in Geneva. His pronouncement there created a sensation throughout the whole world.

SIXTEEN

It was a fortuitous circumstance that in September 1932, it was the turn of Ireland, the newly admitted member of the League of Nations to preside over the thirteenth meeting of the Assembly in Geneva. Eamon de Valera found himself in a new and strange environment. This was no Irish gathering over which he presided. Facing him were the representatives of 56 nations embracing the whole civilized world, with the notable exceptions of the United States, Germany, Japan and Brazil.

Every eye in the chamber was on de Valera as he rose to speak. Everyone was anxious to hear what this fiery-eyed revolutionary, as the British press had told them he was, would say. In all previous opening meetings of the Assembly, the Chairman had simply read the speech prepared for him by the Secretariat. Would the Irish representative meekly conform and do likewise, or would he electrify the Assembly by launching out into an attack on British imperialism?

Dev spoke quietly and deliberately, but what he said in the first few minutes had the attention of every delegate in the Chamber. Almost casually, he pushed aside the speech prepared for him and proceeded to deliver one of his own. This was unprecedented, but so also was what followed. He said that the problem of disarmament, which the Conference had been considering for a year, had made little progress. It fell far short of the desires and expectations of the peoples of the world. The League could not continue in existence if it lost the confidence of the people. It had no sanctions but the force of world opinion. The testing time had come and people were watching to see if the first test would reveal a weakness which would result in the dissolution of the League, or a strength which would enable it to grow and be effective. They should be frank with themselves. There were on all sides complaints, criticism and suspicion. The complaints were that the League was devoting its activities to petty things, while ignoring the major problems that touched the very existence of our peoples. They were saying that the equality of states did not apply in the League in things that mattered and that the smaller states had very little real influence. There was a suspicion abroad that little more than lip service was paid to the fundamental principles on which the League was founded.

Dev spoke for about fifteen minutes. The plain implication in his speech was that the League was being used by the victorious Big Powers in their own selfish interests and that if this was the case, the League was bound to fail. He said,

> The one effective way of silencing criticism of the League, of bringing to its support millions who at present stand aside in apathy or look at its activities with undisguised cynicism, is to show immediately that the Covenant of the League is a solemn pact, the obligations of which no state, great or small, will find it possible to ignore. The only alternative to competitive armaments is the security for national rights which an uncompromising adherence to the principles of the Covenant will afford. The evidence of wars and of the burden of preparatory armaments is of such concern to humanity that no state should be permitted to jeopardise the common interest by selfish action contrary to the Covenant, and no state is powerful enough to stand for long against the League if the governments in the League and their peoples are determined that the Covenant shall be upheld.

He ended his speech by a reference to Ireland.

> Speaking for my own country, I am confident that if we are left free to pursue our own policy we shall succeed not only in securing proper adjustment of our social and economic life, but shall be able to contribute more than our share to human progress throughout the world. I want you to believe that we in Ireland desire peace—peace at home and peace abroad. In spite of opinions you may have formed from misleading reports, I want you to know that our history

is the history of a people who have consistently sought merely to be allowed to lead their own lives in their own way, at peace with their neighbours and the world.

The speech had worldwide repercussions. In the Assembly Hall in Geneva it was received in stony silence. Usually the address of the President to the Assembly was greeted with polite applause, but this earnest and dedicated man had made such an impact on a gathering drilled into polite acceptance of platitudes, that his hearers were almost stunned.

But outside the Assembly Hall and outside Geneva the world was listening and for the first time since the League of Nations had been established, they had heard a real voice raised in that Assembly. The speech was reported on the front pages of the world's newspapers and the editorial comments it evoked placed Dev in the front rank of the world's statesmen.

The *New York Times*, the most influential newspaper on the American continent, said that de Valera had emerged as "the personality of the Session and had revealed himself as the League's strong man."

The *English Review* said, "There is no doubt that in brushing aside the harmless text prepared for him and telling the League of Nations what he thought of it, the Fianna Fáil leader voiced the views of millions of people all over the world."

The *Daily Herald* correspondent in Geneva said, "It was the best speech I have ever heard at the League Assembly and that is the opinion of almost every journalist with whom I have spoken."

The London *Daily Express* in a report headed "Geneva stunned by de Valera's onslaught" said that "the Irish leader had refused to repeat the customary rigmarole of pious platitudes drafted for him."

In almost every European capital, national newspapers added to the tributes that Dev's speech had evoked. He was hailed not merely as a great national leader, but as a world statesman of the first rank. No longer could the British brand him as a wild-eyed visionary who claimed the impossible. He had at last been recognised by all the world outside Great Britain as a statesman far greater than anyone they had produced, a man who stood high in the counsels of the nations of the world.

He was to ascend even higher in those counsels. His words in 1932 had failed to avert the trend towards war which everybody feared. Three times thereafter he appeared in the Assembly of the League and on each occasion he tried to head off the war which was in the offing. If he had been listened to and his advice had been taken, the world might have been saved from a terrible disaster.

On one occasion at a League session he seemed to lose his temper. The question under discussion was whether Russia should be admitted to League membership. Dev had made an eloquent appeal to the Russians to grant religious freedom to all the people within her borders, and had stated that he himself was in favour of admission. But the great powers which dominated the League were set on bargaining and the delegates were left guessing for many days while the bargainers deliberated the question in secret.

At last Dev cut loose. He reminded the delegates that the conception of the League was open covenants, openly arrived at and he denounced "the hotel room diplomacy" which was going on behind closed doors while the vast majority of the delegates were left twiddling their thumbs. He said that the League had a dignity to maintain and so had the member nations of the League.

"The procedure to be adopted," he said, "should not be made a matter for consideration in hotel rooms where the voice of those delegates who might oppose Russia's entry would not be heard. The question should be openly and frankly faced."

He said that the country he represented, if one considered its political and religious ideals, was as far apart as the Poles from Soviet Russia, but he was willing to take the responsibility of saying openly and frankly that he would vote for the entry of Russia because of the considerations involved. He appealed to the Assembly to countenance nothing that would give an impression of intrigue. He realised that things that counted most in human life were being attacked in Russia. Hundreds of millions of Christians believed that to deprive a man of his religion was to deprive life of its meaning. He appealed to the Russians to guarantee the liberty of conscience and the freedom of worship, which they had guaranteed to American citizens, to all other nationalities and to their own people. Such a guarantee freely and openly given in the Assembly would be worth more than any extracted as a result of bargaining behind closed doors in a hotel room.

On two other occasions in the League he found himself torn between conflicting loyalties. The first was when Italy invaded Ethiopia. In spite of the age-long friendly ties that had existed between Italy and Ireland, he voted for sanctions against Italy as the aggressor. The second was during the Spanish Civil War. The land of his forbears was in the throes of a bloody war of brothers. Almost the whole of the leaders of the Church, of which he is an ardent and devoted member, were on the side of Franco and, indeed, there was an Irish brigade organised to fight on Franco's side, but de Valera stood firm by the League's decision of non-intervention. Only a man of iron will and determination could have taken such a stand in the circumstances.

If there had been more men like him in the Geneva Assembly, the League would not have died as ignominiously as it did and Europe and the world would have been spared the horrors of the Second World War.

SEVENTEEN

By the end of 1936 de Valera had succeeded in eliminating the more obnoxious features of the Treaty of 1922. He had got rid of the Oath of Allegiance and the right of appeal from Irish courts to the British Privy Council. He had won back the occupied ports of Lough Swilly, Berehaven and Cobh, and persuaded the British to relinquish the right conceded to them in the Treaty to occupy any and all Irish ports in time of war or strained relations. It cannot be emphasised too often that by this last achievement he had saved Ireland from being involved in the Second World War.

As yet he had not got rid of the Governor General, but with the connivance of his old friend Donal O'Buckley, whom he had appointed to that post, he had relegated the position to one of relative obscurity as a prior step to abolishing the post entirely.

The abdication of King Edward VIII gave him the opportunity he sought. On the day following the abdication he introduced in the Dáil the External Relations Act which abolished the post of Governor General and removed from the Constitution the King and all the King's functions in Ireland, internal and external. Thus, within four years of his taking office, he had succeeded in removing all the obnoxious clauses in the Free State Constitution. On the following day he introduced a Bill authorising the British King to act for Ireland in external affairs on the advice of the Irish government. This tenuous link with the British Commonwealth was retained in the hope that it might make easier a solution of the Partition problem.

This legislation paved the way for the new Constitution on the drafting of which he had been working for a whole year. Historians of the future may hold that it was his greatest achievement. The document was drawn up not merely for the twenty-six counties, but for the whole Irish nation. Its content throughout is permeated with the exalted spirit of the preamble:

> In the name of the Most Holy Trinity, from Whom is all authority, and to Whom, as our final end, all actions both of men and States must be referred,
>
> We, the people of Éire,
>
> Humbly acknowledging all our obligations to the Divine Lord, Jesus Christ, Who sustained our fathers through centuries of trial,
>
> Gratefully remembering their heroic and unremitting struggle to regain the rightful independence of our Nation,
>
> And seeking to promote the common good, with due observance of Prudence, Justice and Charity, so that the dignity and freedom of the individual may be assured, true social order attained, the unity of our country restored, and concord established with other nations,
>
> Do hereby adopt, enact, and give to ourselves this Constitution.

A commentator said that in this day and age a charter for the people containing such language and such sentiments could have come only from Ireland. He might have said, with equal truth, that it could have come only from the mind and heart of Eamon de Valera.

Prior to the outbreak of the Second World War, Dev had declared many times that in the event of such a conflict Ireland would remain neutral. He had also stated many times that in such a case Ireland would not allow her territory to be used as a base for an attack on England. How he managed to be loyal to both those promises and the measures he took to honour them involved endless vigilance which continued every day the war lasted. Towards the end of 1938 he projected an extensive visit to America, which involved a journey to the main U.S. cities and was to last several weeks. A national welcoming committee had been formed in New York with sub-committees in every city from New York to California and from Buffalo in New York State to Miami in Florida.

On the eve of the projected tour, the preparations for which had taken months of organisational work, it was cancelled, the reason being that the British government had decided to extend the Conscription Act to the six counties. Dev held that this was a violation of the rights of Irish nationals and he decided to remain in Ireland to contest the measure. He said to the British government, "We claim the whole of Ireland as national territory. The conscription of Irishmen we will regard as an act of aggression." In the upshot, the proposed legislation was withdrawn. It was the second time that Dev had come to the aid of the North and averted Conscription in that area, but it was not the last time he was to show his concern for his countrymen in that area, for when Belfast was bombed by the Germans during the war and the fires were raging in that city, he ordered the Dublin Fire Brigade to Belfast to quench the fires. He knew well that German bombers considered that they were within their rights in bombing Belfast, which was in their view and in that of the British, British territory, but he held that the Irish had a viewpoint as well and that was that the people of Belfast were our people and that we had a perfect right to come to their assistance.

When the guns opened fire, however, on 1 September 1939, to start the Second World War, de Valera found himself bombarded from all sides. He had during the previous year made gigantic strides to come to terms with the I.R.A. in an attempt to obtain national unity in face of the terrible threat of the European war. He had a secret interview with Sean Russell, the Chief of the I.R.A., only to find that he could get nowhere. The I.R.A. Chief insisted on a course which would have meant war with England. In fact, the I.R.A. formally sent to Lord Halifax, the British Foreign Minister, an ultimatum signed by Russell declaring war against Britain unless British forces were withdrawn from the North and soon thereafter the I.R.A. terroristic campaign began in England. In this campaign many perfectly innocent civilians lost their lives. Not only that, but the activities of the I.R.A. were redoubled in Ireland, at a time when Hitler's legions were overrunning Norway, Holland, and Belgium. It soon became apparent that the I.R.A. were acting in concert with the German High Command, with a view to a Nazi invasion. Several parachutists from Germany were dropped in Ireland and most of them were immediately arrested. One, however, Hermann Goertz, remained at large for over a year, during which he kept in close touch with the I.R.A. and had at least one interview with Von Hempel, the German Minister. Actually and unbelievably, Von Hempel called on Dev to ask him if he would welcome German help. We have not been told what Dev's reply was, but with the example of Norway, Belgium, and Denmark before him, we can guess.

At this time there were few people who would believe that Dev could maintain Irish neutrality, particularly as the pressure from Britain to allow her the use of Irish territory and Irish ports increased from day to day. Churchill privately had his military chiefs prepare a plan by which a division could be landed in Ireland in the shortest possible time and he told the House of Commons that "the fact that we cannot use the south and west coasts of Ireland to refuel our flotillas and aircraft is a most heavy and grievous burden."

Dev replied that he would not make Ireland a cockpit of war and see his people slaughtered and their homes levelled. He called for recruits for the defence forces and the call was responded to nobly. Ultimately there were no fewer than 250,000 enrolled in the various security forces.

After America entered the war, the pressure from the Allies' side increased. The Americans could not understand why in such a conflict Ireland should stand aside. Dev's answer was that he had given ample notice that if the war occurred, Ireland would remain neutral and that it was all very well for America, a country which was so great and strong that it could recover from the devastation of war whatever happened, but that for a small country like Ireland the intervention in a war between such leviathans might be the end.

On the eve of the allied invasion of Europe, de Valera received a direct demand from the American government. The American Minister, David Grey, called on him with a note from President Roosevelt requesting that the German and Japanese representatives in Dublin be sent home on the grounds that the Axis agents enjoyed almost unrestricted opportunities of transmitting information of vital importance to Germany.

This request, if granted, would have meant breaking off diplomatic relations with the Axis powers and would have meant the end of neutrality. Dev replied with a diplomatically worded refusal. Perhaps not in any time in the modern history of nations is there a more courageous instance of a small nation standing up to such an array of big powers as the Allies presented in 1944 on the eve of victory.

When the bells of victory rang out for the Allies on 7 May 1945, it was clear in the minds of his countrymen that he was a David who had faced Goliath. He had saved his country from involvement in the greatest holocaust of all time.

No man other than Dev could have done it.

EIGHTEEN

For a man who has in the course of his own lifetime become an institution, the way is always difficult and sometimes, indeed, well nigh impossible. Dev was only 36 years old when he became the leader of his people. In the course of one short year in 1918, he was elected President of the newly created Parliament of Ireland, Dáil Eireann, President of the only effective political organisation of the day, Sinn Féin, and President of the fighting force which was to become the Army of the Republic, the Irish Volunteers.

Any young man given such power might have succumbed to its lures and become a tyrant, or a dictator. Instead, in spite of his exalted position and in spite of the fact that he has been so long the voice of his people, not merely at home but in the counsels of the nations of the world, Dev has remained just the modest and unspoiled man, who is proud of the fact that he comes of peasant stock and that he was brought up in a labourer's cottage in Bruree, County Limerick. It is this quality in him which evokes the comparison with Abraham Lincoln.

Lloyd George said of him, "he will never change" and this is as true of him today as when the words were spoken 25 years ago. He will never change on fundamentals.

When the war in Europe appeared to be coming to an end, the victors decided to go after war criminals, tooth and nail. They remembered that after the First World War, the Kaiser had sought and found asylum in Holland. They feared that the war criminals (meaning, of course, the Germans and Italians and not at all the Russians) might seek asylum in a neutral country. They demanded that the neutral nations should give guarantees that they would not harbour war criminals. All of the neutrals were warned that if any shelter or assistance or protection were given to the war criminals, it would be regarded as a "violation of the principles for which the United Nations were fighting and which they were determined to carry into effect by every means in their power."

Mr. Cordell Hull, the American Secretary of State, lists the neutral nations so approached. They were Switzerland, Spain, Portugal, Sweden, Turkey, Argentina, and Ireland. One and all of them sought to maintain the right of asylum that had been held sacred for thousands of years. As a result of continued pressure, all of them bowed before the threat of the big stick—all but one. Only Ireland held out. Dev told the Americans that he would not yield. He said that his government was unable to give assurances that would render it impossible for it to exercise its right to grant asylum should justice, charity or the honour or the interest of the nation so require. The American State Department, in an angry reply, renewed their demand, but got no further.

Alone of all the neutrals, Ireland stood by the ancient right of asylum and defied the United Nations on that point. Dev knew that right was on his side, and right transcended all other considerations.

Perhaps it is this characteristic of his more than any other which has so endeared him to his fellow countrymen, his iron determination to stand by the right under any and all circumstances. Neither threats nor cajolery will lure him from the path of right and justice. On the occasion of the Abyssinian crisis, in spite of the strong ties which had always existed between Italy and Ireland, he had not hesitated to invoke sanctions against Italy for her aggression against the tiny African state. In the Spanish Civil War he had stood by the League's decision not to intervene although almost overwhelming forces were brought to bear on him to declare in favour of Franco. In the case of the United States, after the attack on Pearl Harbour, he had said that his heart would have to be made of stone if he felt nothing after all America had done for

Ireland, and yet when American troops landed at Derry, he at once sent a formal protest to Washington on this violation of Irish territory. Even at the hands of such a friendly country as the United States, he would not countenance a condonation of the partition of Ireland.

Who amongst us who listened in to Radio Éireann on 16 May 1945 will ever forget the voice of Eamon de Valera in his famous reply to Winston Churchill's victory message to the world? The British Prime Minister, in the course of his address, had said:

> Owing to the action of Mr. de Valera so much at variance with the temper and instinct of Southern Irishmen who hastened to the battle front to prove their ancient valour, the approaches which the southern Irish ports and airfields could so easily have guarded were closed by the hostile aircrafts and U boats.
>
> This was indeed a deadly moment in our life, and if it had not been for the loyalty and friendship of Northern Ireland, we should have been forced to come to close quarters with Mr. de Valera or perish forever from the earth.
>
> However . . . we left the de Valera government to frolic with the German and later with the Japanese representatives to their hearts' content.

The studied insult in the words, beset with half-truths and cheap sneers, hit hard. The Irish people were furious and when it was announced that Dev would reply from Radio Éireann, all Ireland listened in.

Dev spoke quietly and dispassionately. He said he knew the reply he would have given to Churchill a quarter of a century earlier, but he did not wish to add any fuel to the flames of hatred and passion. He said that Mr. Churchill had made it clear that in certain circumstances he would have violated Irish neutrality and that he would have justified his action by Britain's necessity. Could Mr. Churchill not see that in this case Britain's necessity would have become a moral code under which other people's rights were not to count? Surely that was at the root of the war and if it was accepted as a code, no small nation adjoining a great power could go its way in peace. Suppose, he said, that Germany had invaded England and had partitioned that country and occupied six of its counties, would Mr. Churchill lead such a partitioned England in a crusade with Germany, or would he feel a sense of shame if such a partitioned England remained neutral in a great war in which Germany was engaged?

Mr. Churchill, he said, was proud of Britain's stand alone after the fall of France. Could he not be generous enough to acknowledge that Ireland, a small nation, had stood alone against aggression not for a year, or two, but for several hundred years during which she had endured spoliations, famines and massacres in endless succession, a small nation that could never accept defeat and had never surrendered her soul. Mr. Churchill was justly proud of his nation's perseverance against heavy odds. We in Ireland are still prouder of our people's perseverance for freedom through the centuries. Many a time in the past there appeared little hope, except that hope to which Mr. Churchill referred, that by standing fast a time would come when, to quote his own words, "the tyrant would make some ghastly mistake which would alter the whole balance of the struggle." Dev said that when he was a younger man he had prayed even for that, but now he had a vision of a nobler and better ending, better for both our peoples and for the future of mankind. For that he had long been working. He regretted that it was not to this nobler purpose that Mr. Churchill was lending his hand. Instead, by the abuse of a people who had done him no wrong, he was trying to find an excuse for continuing the injustice of the mutilation of Ireland's territory.

The commentators of the day record the tremendous impact that this speech had on public opinion.

"Here," said one of them, "was a statesman who scorned the petty ways of political debate and who displayed an unfailing sense of the balance of the rights and obligations of nations."

There was no reply from the British side.

When Dev said he had long been working towards a nobler and better ending to the problem of partition, the last remaining political objective of Irish nationalism, he was speaking the simple truth. In 1938 in his negotiations with Neville Chamberlain he thought for a while that he was on the threshold of success, but circumstances outside his control dashed his hopes. He had ruled out force as a means to that end. Indeed, he told the Fianna Fáil Ard-Fheis, in November 1955, that the ideal of the Republican movement had always been quite the opposite to that of those who advocated force. The Republican picture of the free Ireland to be achieved was one in which all sections of the people on this island lived in harmony, each jealous of the nation's honour, proud of its past and striving in rivalry with the others to advance the common welfare. That ideal could not be achieved by the exercise of force. Even if it were militarily successful, we would lack the harmony essential to our ideal.

Those are the words of a statesman and not of a mere politician. The speech shows that his stature has grown with the years. If anyone thinks there is a waning of his mental powers or of his intellectual vigour, they have only to read the forceful, clear, and logical reply that he made in Ennis on 9 March of this year to Prime Minister Macmillan's ill-timed and ill-informed statement in Belfast on the partition issue.

The fact is that he is as mentally alert as ever and, considering his 77 years, he is physically fit above the average. But failing eyesight, which would be a terrible handicap to anyone, has become an intolerable burden for a man who has to undergo the heavy day-to-day routine of political leadership. And so he has to relinquish his position as Taoiseach.

It is, however, a consolation, to know that his successor will have the wise guidance of the greatest political genius—perhaps the greatest statesman—which our country has ever produced.

Editorial Note: After stepping down as Prime Minister in 1959, Eamon de Valera served as President of Ireland from 1959 to 1973. He died in 1975 at the age of 93.